Channeling Grace

CARL L. JECH

SERMONS FOR
LENT AND EASTER
(SUNDAYS IN ORDINARY TIME)
CYCLE C GOSPEL TEXTS

C.S.S. Publishing Co., Inc.
Lima, Ohio

CHANNELING GRACE

Copyright © 1988 by
The C.S.S. Publishing Company, Inc.
Lima, Ohio

All rights reserved. No part of this publication may be reproduced, stored in a retrieval system, or transmitted in any form or by any means, electronic, mechanical, photocopying, recording, or otherwise, without the prior permission of the publisher. Inquiries should be addressed to: The C.S.S. Publishing Company, Inc., 628 South Main Street, Lima, Ohio 45804.

Library of Congress Cataloging-in-Publication Data

Jech, Carl L., 1941-
   Channeling grace.

   1. Lenten sermons. 2. Easter — Sermons. 3. Sermons, American. I. Title.
BV4277.J44   1988   252'.62   88-7319
ISBN 1-55673-054-3

8851 / ISBN 1-55673-054-3   PRINTED IN U.S.A.

Table of Contents

Lent

Ash Wednesday	*The Piety That Isn't* *Matthew 6:1-6, 16-21*	7
Lent 1	*What Does It Mean To Believe In Jesus?* *Luke 4:1-13*	11
Lent 2	*Winning Isn't The Only Thing* *. . . It's Irrelevant!* *Luke 9:28-36 and Luke 13:31-35*	16
Lent 3	*Love Over Logic* *Luke 13:1-9*	22
Lent 4	*Save Us From The World Savers* *Luke 15:1-3, 11-32*	30
Lent 5 (Common)	*Love Is Down To Earth* *John 12:1-8*	36
Lent 5 (Lutheran)	*Jesus, Mary, Gustav Mahler,* *Brother Martin and The Magi* *Luke 20:9-19*	42
Lent 5 (Roman Catholic)	*Some Women's Stories* *John 8:1-11*	48
Lent 6 (Passion Sunday)	*Comfort The Disturbed/* *Disturb The Comfortable* *Luke 22:1 — 23:56*	54
Maundy Thursday	*Giving Away The Store* *Luke 22:7-20 and John 13:1-15*	59
Good Friday	*What's Love Got To Do?* *John 19:17-30*	64

Easter

Easter Day	*Will The Real Jesus Christ Arise?* *John 20:1-18*	68
Easter 2	*Colorizing Jesus* *John 20:19-31*	75
Easter 3	*Throw Your Heart At The Sky* *John 21:1-14*	82
Easter 4	*"Give Me Jesus"* *John 10:22-30 (27-30)*	89
Easter 5	*Divine Liturgy, Divine Play,* *Divine Comedy* *John 13:31-35*	95
Easter 6	*Becoming What You Are* *John 14:23-29*	102
Ascension Day/Ascension Sunday	*Jesus Meets* *Buddha and Confucius* *Luke 24:44-53*	108
Easter 7	*The Real Jesus Is* *Channeling Grace* *John 17:20-26*	116

In Loving Memory of
Eli Schoenfeld, Gerry Stafford, Jeffrey Dayton,
and my father,
The Rev. Herbert J. S. Jech

Dedication

To my mother and sisters,
Helen, Margaret *and* ***Mary***

About the Author

Carl L. Jech teaches philosophy, religion and humanities at the Foothill/DeAnza Colleges in Palo Alto and Cupertino, California and at the College of Marin in Kentfield, California.

A performing artist, he has appeared as tenor soloist with the Milwaukee Bach Chamber Choir and Orchestra and with numerous San Francisco Bay Area musical organizations. He has sung in many choral groups around the country, including with the Philadelphia Orchestra under the late Eugene Ormandy. He has also performed various roles in productions of the Marin Civic Light Opera, most recently starring as Frederic in *The Pirates of Penzance*. A 1986 performance of Schubert's song cycle *Die Schoene Mullerin* received critical acclaim in the San Francisco press as "genuine artistry." He has also been performing as a magician for many years and has only recently had an opportunity to demonstrate a variety of his talents on Bay Area television.

A native of Minnesota, he graduated from Wartburg College in Waverly, Iowa, and holds the M. Div. degree from Wartburg Theological Seminary and the Th. M. degree from Harvard Divinity School. He has served as pastor at congregations in Michigan and California and was campus pastor at the University of Wisconsin — Whitewater. He is the father of two children, Dawn and Jeffrey.

Jech is the author of a number of journal articles and his first book, *Shadows and Symbols*, was published by C.S.S. Publishing Company in 1985.

Matthew 6:1-6, 16-21 Ash Wednesday

The Piety That Isn't

Beware of practicing your piety before men in order to be seen . . .

(Matthew 6:1a)

The well-known San Francisco newspaper columnist, Herb Caen, recently made a provocative observation when he wrote: "The miracle of Christmas is that it survives those who believe in it too loudly." The Christmas/Epiphany season is now over, and it might be good for us to ponder the significance of Mr. Caen's observation.

Lent is traditionally a time for self-examination. The most common form of such self-examination focuses on our failure to live up to "the high calling of God in Christ Jesus." We assume that we *know* what this calling is all about and that our only problem is failing to follow through on the obvious implications of our faith.

I think Herb Caen's comment should move us to undertake in this series of sermons an unusual, perhaps, but nonetheless valid form of lenten self-examination. Taking a warning cue from Matthew's line "Beware of practicing your piety," we are going to consider the possible errors and sins we commit precisely as the result of *misguided* efforts to live out our piety. To put it another way, we are going to examine some of our fundamental assumptions about the nature of the Christian Good News, the Gospel. Maybe the Gospel is less obvious than we tend to think it is.

We are going to ask whether some forms of "Christian commitment" might actually be a denial of the Gospel and a misrepresentation of what Christian *evangelism* is really supposed to be. Some would even go so far as to say that the word "evangelical" has been spoiled by those whose style of being Christian promotes the wrong kind of narrowness. They would say that the Christian faith is *embarrassed* when God is identified with a particular candidate or party, *embarrassed* by the stark polarization between "liberal" and "conservative" churches over the issues of (1) church doctrine and practice, (2) abortion, (3) church and state issues, (4) interpretation of the Bible, (5) life-styles, and (6) views on morality. In this video age of images, where the outward image is so strong that Michael J. Fox, Tina Turner and Michael Jackson don't even have to say the name Pepsi to sell the product in a commercial, must not we too pay attention to the Gospel's *image*?

Can we ignore these issues and simply practice our piety, simply focus on that which is spiritually uplifting and let the rest slide? Not if we heed the words of Matthew's Gospel! Practicing true piety, true spirituality, is a tricky, challenging thing, and Lent is not a time to look for an easy way out.

It could well be that polarizing or otherwise faulty expressions of our Christian piety have actually worked to drive people away from Christianity. It is likely that much of the popularity of psychics, astrology, certain "cult" phenomena, trance channeling and the like, is the result of mistakes that we Christians have made in the attempt to express our faith. To use a big word, some of our efforts to attract people may be sadly *counterproductive*. Was Shirley MacLaine pushed out on a limb because the Christianity she had known was too dogmatic, too arrogant, too intellectualized or formal — not paying enough attention to her hunger for religious *experience*? By virtually ignoring the other world religions do Christians unintentionally exaggerate the appeal of those religions?

This day, Ash Wednesday, is a day on which some mark their foreheads with ashes — symbolizing repentance, symbolizing the Cross, symbolizing our mortality (often with the words: "Remember that you are dust and to dust you shall return"). No doubt some people do not follow this custom because they have noticed that it seems to conflict with Matthew's words in the text for this day, his words about not making a show of your piety in public. It could be argued that since this form of piety emphasizes humility, it can't possibly be interpreted as "showing off." But in this sermon, Jesus is referring precisely to those who disfigure their faces as a way of showing how humble they are. Now most of us don't stand on street corners and many of us do not mark our foreheads with ashes, but in a variety of subtle ways we may well be guilty of "practicing our piety before men," contrary to the Spirit of Jesus.

We Christians have been given a difficult challenge. We have been challenged to witness to our faith without being "triumphalistic," without being boastful about our beliefs, our convictions, our morality. It's a tough challenge and it is not going to be easy to talk about it. But this is Lent. Let us *really* examine ourselves.

"Amazing Grace . . . that saved a wretch like me." (John Newton)

The point is not that we aren't to practice any piety at all. The point is that we need to be careful how we go about being pious. To say, for example that "God helps those who help themselves" may express an important truth about self-reliance; but if the phrase is quoted as an excuse for not helping those in need, then it is not a good thought. Likewise, the insight suggested by the question "Whoever said life is fair?" can help us face the hard realities of life; but if the same question is used as an excuse for not getting involved in the struggle to create social justice in the world, then the truth is being mishandled. The mystic, Bernard of Clairvaux, said that "only one who is poor should praise poverty." Economic poverty may help us keep our priorities straight — may make us more aware of the real treasures of life — but for an affluent person to praise poverty could be, again, to make an excuse for not being concerned about the plight of the poor.

Those who have experienced the "Amazing Grace" of God can reflect on how, without that grace, they felt like lost wretches: but they should not go around labeling other people as lost and wretched. It is one thing to say that *I* was lost or spiritually blind, but it is quite another thing, quite inappropriate, for me to call others lost, blind or wretched. To do so would be not evangelistic, but *arrogant*. Watching the "Church Lady" on *Saturday Night Live* reminds, us that the line between true evangelism and holier-than-thou self-righteousness is extremely thin, but oh so important. It may be easier to confess other people's sins, but we can only confess our own. (It's easier, but wrong, to confess the sins to which we are not tempted.) Just as a joke can be funny or offensive depending on the spirit in which it is told and taken, so an expression of our piety (like confession) can be true and lovely, or false and ugly, depending on the spirit in which it is conveyed. Ironically, to be preoccupied with other people's sins is itself the basic sin of self-righteous self-centeredness!

Christians are given the difficult challenge of expressing a piety that isn't pious in a self-righteous, self-important way! As we move through this lenten season we will be using the image of "channeling grace" to describe what a truly "evangelical mentality" is all about. As channels of God's grace we will learn how to have convictions without being bigoted or closed-minded, how to be angry at injustice without being self-righteous, how to share faith without "practicing our piety before men." This lenten season of penitence calls us not to wallow in sin-consciousness but to make a commitment to renewal and reform. The Greek word for repentance means "to change one's mind." Let us do some truly radical mind-changing. Let us rethink what it means to be *evangelical*!

We began by quoting Herb Caen's comment about "those who believe in Christmas too loudly." The great preacher Harry Emerson Fosdick similarly gave us a witty nudge toward the piety that isn't, when he said that vital faith is a treasure like good music . . . "It needs no defense, only rendition. A wrangling controversy in support of religion," said Fosdick, "is as if the members of the orchestra should beat folks over the head with their violins to prove that the music is beautiful."

The amazing truth is that by going easy on the piety, by not beating folks over the head with the Bible, we become much more effective channels of God's grace. The piety that isn't pious is the true piety! Let us celebrate and, in the weeks to come, contemplate this amazing paradox of God's grace!

Luke 4:1-13 *Lent 1*

What Does It Mean to Believe in Jesus?

And the devil took him up and showed him all the kingdoms of the world in a moment of time, and said to him, "To you I will give all this authority and their glory . . ."

(Luke 4:5-6a)

    This text may well be the most shocking passage in the entire New Testament! Why? Because it pictures *the devil* as believing that Jesus should have "the power and the glory for ever and ever!" The book of *James* echoes this theme by saying that "even the demons believe — and shudder." (James 2:19b) As Christians we usually assume that our mission is to get people to believe in Jesus. But more and more I think we must face the issue of *what kind* of belief in Jesus! What does it *mean* to believe in Jesus? In this story, the devil "believes" in Jesus. But it is the wrong kind of belief!
    A major church periodical recently printed this quotation from Vittorio Messori: "Christianity in no way sees itself as one of the religions; it sees itself as the sufficient and definitive revelation of God in history. At the heart of Christian faith there is not just another religious theory; there is the Good News about Jesus." In 1986 the vice president of the American Lutheran Church, Dr. Lloyd Svendsbye, was asked to respond to a charge that Lutheran publications had published writings which "denied that Jesus was the only way to salvation." His answer was that those who deny faith in Christ as the only way to salvation should be disciplined. That same year the cover of a major seminary's Christmas mailing emblazoned the prayer "Savior of the Nations, Come!" Do we have here examples of believing in Jesus too loudly? I think we have to ask what it *means* to believe that "Jesus is the only way to salvation." Could we

be trying to give Jesus the very kind of authority and glory that Jesus himself rejects in this story of his temptation?

In 1982, James Burtness, a professor at Luther Northwestern Theological Seminary in Saint Paul, Minnesota, wrote a provocative article entitled "Does Anyone Out There Care Anymore Whether People Believe in Jesus?" In that article he complained about a post-Auschwitz refusal on the part of some Christians "to state clearly to Jewish people the claim of Jesus to be the Messiah . . ." and he accused such Christians of making belief in Jesus "optional." While professor Burtness did recognize the arrogance of equating Christianity with Western values and culture, he apparently does not believe that it is arrogant to ask all people of all religions to "accept Jesus."

Dr. Burtness does conclude, however, that "from time to time we need to ask whether our perspective requires some adjustment. No one should claim to be entirely right about Jesus," he warns. I take this to mean that we must continually be asking ourselves what it *means* to believe in Jesus. The hard question we are asking ourselves is whether some have stopped caring about believing in Jesus precisely because others have believed in Jesus in the wrong ways.

"How Sweet the Name of Jesus Sounds . . . Filled with Boundless Stores of Grace." (John Newton)

At this point you may want to protest that it is impossible to believe in Jesus "too much." After all, doesn't the New Testament say that "there is salvation in no one else, for there is no other name under heaven given among men by which we must be saved" besides the name of Jesus? (Acts 4:12) If Jesus is "the name which is above every name, that at the name of Jesus every knee should bow" (Philippians 2:9-10), why and how can it be a temptation from the devil for Jesus to want authority and glory over all nations?

The answer to these questions is to be found by focusing on the meaning of this name *Jesus* itself! The name *Jesus* is the same as the name *Joshua*. The name *means* "God will deliver," "God will heal," "God will save." Therefore, to believe in Jesus means, simply, to believe that *salvation is God's doing*! We may be a long way from fully understanding what *salvation* means, but what we do know is that salvation is God's business, God's prerogative, and not ours! It is not up to us to save people, to win people, to judge people.

To say that the only way to be saved is through the *name* of Jesus is to say that only God has the answers to questions about who is saved. To proclaim that this is the *only way* to be saved sounds narrow and exclusive. But, in fact, it is as broad and open as all outdoors! If the only way to be saved is by God (that is, in the name *Jesus*), then who are we to put limits on who God can save? It is not up to us to say whether Jews or Hindus or, for that matter, atheists, can be saved — because God alone is in charge of salvation. The Christian is called to contemplate and share the mystery of God's saving grace. Our calling is not so much "to get everyone to believe in Jesus" as it is *to engage the world in dialogue about what it means to believe that God alone is totally in charge of our "salvation,"* indeed, that God alone knows what salvation itself really means! John Newton expresses beautifully the true meaning of Jesus' name in his hymn: "How sweet the name of Jesus sounds in a believer's ear! . . . Dear Name! . . . filled with boundless stores of grace."

According to the story of our text, the devil's belief in Jesus is inadequate because it puts the wrong kind of emphasis on the personal glory of Jesus. The New Testament as a whole pictures a Jesus who is humble, giving, self-emptying! Jesus, according to an early Christian hymn, "did not count equality with God a thing to be grasped, but emptied himself . . . humbled himself and became obedient unto death, even death on a cross. Therefore God has highly exalted him and bestowed on him the name which is above every name, that at the name of Jesus every knee should bow . . ." (Philippians 2) Jesus is not a Christ who makes great claims, but a Christ, a Messiah, an "anointed one," who is absolutely humble and self-giving. The entire Gospel of Luke is an ode to humility. The Christmas story in Luke 2 virtually says that we should *worship* humility! Jesus is the kind of Messiah who empties himself and relates first and foremost to the poor and the outcasts. Jesus is not concerned with his own status. He is content to be an open channel of God's grace. His specialness is his utterly down-to-earth rejection of any self-glorification. Our "witness" to this Jesus must be equally humble! Such humility is not easy.

Do you remember the satirical ditty that kids used to sing? — "I don't care if it rains or freezes, 'long as I have my plastic Jesus fastened to the dashboard of my car." We are sorely tempted to make Jesus into an all-too-human idol or lucky charm. This story of Jesus' temptation tells us that for Jesus to have claimed all power and glory in such crass, human terms would have been demonic. The classical theology of our Christian tradition has concluded that Jesus is "divine" only in the paradoxical sense that he points away from himself to God, away from himself to that which transcends human notions of divinity! When we read in 2 Corinthians 5:16 that we are not to regard Christ from a human point of view, we are being told that "Jesus" is as much a symbol as he is a person that we must resist the temptation to assume that we know everything there is to know about "Jesus." The book of Genesis says that human beings are made in the image of God. But at the same time it also immediately tells us that to want to be "like God" (Genesis 3:5) is a temptation from the devil. Clearly, if being "in the image of God" and being "like God" are *not* the same thing, equally fine distinctions are in order when we talk about "the divinity of Jesus." Jesus resisted the *temptation* to claim divinity!

Many critics down through the ages have complained that Saint Paul (Saul of Tarsus) took the simple religion *of* Jesus and turned it into a complicated and idolatrous religion *about* Jesus. They would be right, perhaps, *if* Paul had pictured Jesus as the kind of Lord who is a glorious idol that serves us like a lucky charm. But Paul says that he wants to know nothing "except Jesus Christ and him crucified." (1 Corinthians 2:2) In other words, his theology of Jesus is a theology of the utter simplicity and humility of Jesus. Paul's writing may become complex and abstract, but his emphasis on trust in God's grace is fundamentally simple and never arrogant. The message of Jesus as the Messiah always meant for Paul an emphasis on what God is doing in the world, not on *our* efforts or works. There is absolutely no place for Christian "boasting" of any kind! We are not to believe "too loudly."

Paradoxically, precisely because Paul recognized that the life story of Jesus was a symbol for the radical, amazing, saving grace of God, he had to take the *person* of Jesus very seriously. It was clear to him that Jesus was not merely an abstract symbol for some nebulous concept of "grace." Regarding Jesus from more than a human point of view did not mean regarding him from *less* than a human point of view. One thing the Christian faith clearly points to is an ultimate, mysterious synthesis of spiritual and physical. Belief in the resurrection is one form of this faith. Speaking of Jesus as both human and yet more than human is another form of this faith. Jesus has a physical and historical dimension, but is also more than, and other than, a merely physical and historical person. Jesus is spiritual, but more than, and other than, merely spiritual. When we speak of "Jesus," or for that matter, on the other hand, of the "devil," we are referring to a greater reality than we can understand. But we know *enough* when we know that to believe in *the sweet name of Jesus* is to acknowledge the absolutely unlimited, amazing, saving Grace of God which is stronger than any form of evil! Such faith gives no one any grounds for religious arrogance, theological pride or spiritual holier-than-thou-ism.

True belief in the name of Jesus gives us a wonderful freedom from the burden of feeling that our faith is superior, freedom from the burden of pretending to be humble when we are actually being theologically arrogant. Put more positively, true belief in the meaning of the name "Jesus" frees us *for* honest and open dialogue with people of all religious faiths and with people who are skeptical of religion. Evangelists whose misguided faith in Jesus makes them unwilling and/or unable to listen to the insights of other belief systems do not turn out to be effective witnesses to the name of Jesus. They will be trying to control the grace of God rather than acting as open channels of God's grace as revealed in Jesus.

The grace of God as shown to us in Luke's stories of Jesus is not interested in power, authority and glory. It's message is that a seed cannot grow unless it falls in the ground and "dies." A diamond isn't beautiful until it is cut. As the channel of God's grace, Jesus reminds us of an insight captured beautifully also in a Rodgers and Hammerstein song from *The Sound of Music*. "Love isn't love, 'til you give it away."

Jesus was tempted to hoard love and power for himself. But, instead, he gave it — and gives it — away!

Luke 9:28-36 (L)
Luke 13:31-35 (C, RC)

Lent 2

Winning Isn't the Only Thing . . . It's Irrelevant

Moses and Elijah . . . appeared in glory and spoke of his departure which he was to accomplish at Jerusalem. (Luke 9:31) *"O Jerusalem, Jerusalem . . . How often would I have gathered your children together as a hen gathers her brood under her wings, and you would not!"*

(Luke 13:34)

The Green Bay Packer football coach, Vince Lombardi, is credited with the declaration: "Winning isn't everything . . . It's the *only* thing!" Now from the very limited perspective of a professional football coach there may be an element of truth in this statement. But in the broader arenas of life, winning is *not* the only thing. Winning is often irrelevant! The Gospel stories of Jesus are not stories about winning! Another pithy statement of questionable taste but containing a valid insight has dubbed Jesus "a flop at 33." Jesus is not pictured as one who wants to win at any cost. When the rich ruler walks away from the invitation to follow him (Luke 18:18-27), Jesus does not run after the man. Lamenting the plight of the wealthy, the winners, Jesus let's him go.

Life is more about love than it is about winning, and love often means letting go. Newspaper advice columns remind the romantically inclined not to pursue the object of their affections too ardently. More than one writer has quoted the axiom which says that "indifference is the greatest aphrodisiac." World literature is full of stories of parents who lost the love and affection of their children by holding on too tightly, by stubbornly attempting to win the argument about their child's choice of career, lifestyle, marriage partner. The story of Romeo and Juliet, of course, is the classic example of families wanting to hold their own and win at all costs, only to end up losing what is most precious to them.

While the story of the transfiguration of Jesus has its element of glory, its hint of the resurrection of Jesus, it is also a story about the disciples' failure to understand the true nature of what it was that Jesus "was to accomplish at Jerusalem." The Gospels are full of incidents in which people mistakenly expect Jesus to "be a winner."

We are in the process of looking at ways in which our efforts at evangelism may be similarly mistaken. I do not mean to pick on any one group, but sometimes it takes a specific example to highlight the problem we are addressing. The Gideon society provides a wonderful service by making Bibles available in jails, motels, nursing homes — all over the world. But when Gideons and others say that it is their basic goal to "*win* others for Christ," it could well mean that we are continuing to misunderstand Jesus, that we continue to "not know what we say." (Luke 9:33) We need to be more careful in the words we use to witness. Careless terminology can corrupt our message. Suppose we alter a phrase: "Sticks and stones may break one's bones, but words can wound the spirit."

In the paragraph just before the transfiguration story, Luke has Jesus tell his disciples that the Gospel is not about winning but about *losing*! Traditional incarnational theology says that Jesus gave away everything in order to become human. The story of Jesus is the story of God taking the risk of getting involved, of God letting go of the power and the glory in favor of love and giving!

Perhaps the most careless and misleading terminology we slip into, next to the language of "winning," is the rhetoric that emphasizes the "claims of Christ!" During the Easter season we will discuss the problems with this "claims" terminology at greater length, but for now it is enough to remind ourselves that the New Testament is a complex reflection of the *long process* whereby Jesus comes to be understood as a unique version of "the Christ," the anointed one, the Messiah. To some degree the Gospels all seem to assume that Jesus knows from the outset that he is "the Christ," but it is also clear that the Gospels themselves are the result of considerable after-the-fact interpretation of the meaning of the life of Jesus. Christianity was a complex *movement* and was not based simply on a few direct "claims" made by or about Jesus. To the degree that Jesus or the New Testament writers "claimed" the title of "Christ," they rather consistently did so in a most reluctant manner! In Mark's Gospel, for example, there is the "Messianic Secret" — Jesus is pictured over and over again as cautioning his disciples against noising it abroad that he is the Christ. As we mentioned in the previous sermon, one of the reasons for this is clearly the desire of the Christian movement to give an entirely new *and humble* slant to the concept of the Messiah. There was a great deal of religious/theological ferment at this period in history, and the Christian idea of a Messiah, a Christ, who suffers and gives, and lets go, had to compete with many more glamorous forms of religious belief.

Evangelists who say that the choice people have is between accepting the claims of Christ or calling Jesus a liar, are really just bragging that their particular interpretation of Jesus is beyond question. To put it in classical terms, they are claiming that their "Christology" is the only valid way of understanding the New Testament — quite a grandiose claim when we realize that the New Testament itself presents a variety of Christologies. So it is both arrogant and naive to say that either Jesus was right or he was crazy.

To believe in Jesus is precisely to renounce the style and the substance of arrogant claims. When we are down and out we may like to think of the Gospel as a way of gaining control, certainty and security in our lives. But the Gospel of Jesus is not a "gospel of *having*" — of having all the answers and all the ready-made spiritual resources. Jesus teaches us, rather, not to be afraid of our neediness! The good news is that, in Jesus, we see how, in our own lives, we can combine the ultimate in spiritual humility on the one hand with a confident, hopeful openness to the future on the other.

As Christians we are not called to sell people on the claims of Christ, are not commissioned to create a narrow in-group that divides the world into "us and them." Recently, a representative of Christian charismatics suggested that it would be a great gift for the 2000th birthday of Jesus if we would strive to make half the world Christian by the turn of the century. I seriously wonder if such a numbers-conscious "wave of evangelism" would be in keeping with the spirit of Jesus. It would be more likely to come off as an insensitive hard-sell in a world full of "sales people" of many kinds who don't really care about the well-being of the "customer."

The perhaps startling realization that should be dawning on us at this point is that we must not do "mission work" because we think people are lost unless we "win" them! Evangelism in this spirit is both arrogant and negative. We do evangelism, rather, simply because we sense the overwhelming importance of God's grace! Our mission is not to control and dispense grace but to channel it. The sacraments likewise are channels of God's grace. The church is indeed well-described not so much as an organization but as a *movement*, like a permeating salt or leaven, which channels God's free and unconditional grace to a world that can never have too much of that grace.

"To tell the old, old story of Jesus and his love." (Katherine Hankey)

But you may want to ask again, why trudge off to the ends of the earth doing mission work if you don't believe in the universal claims of Christ as Savior and Messiah — if you think that Jesus was just another great man or prophet with no unique claim on the hearts of humankind?

The answer is that the point of this sermon is *not* to deny that Jesus is the Messiah, the Christ. The point is that Jesus represents precisely a new interpretation — a new understanding — of what it *means* to be the Christ, the Savior! The Christ is not a glorious maker of arrogant claims, but a humble channel of the free grace of God. We do not go to the ends of the earth to tell the story of Jesus as the Messiah because we believe everyone who doesn't accept our version of Christianity is lost, but because we believe simply that the message of God's love and grace is worth telling! Our motivation is basically positive rather than negative — not to save the lost, but to tell Good News. Stories about a messenger whose name means "God will save" are indeed a priceless treasure. We spoil the story if we overlay it with heavyhanded, arrogant claims. Jesus as Savior saves us precisely from believing that it is up to us to save ourselves and the world, from believing that we must be winners in order to have worth.

It does seem to be flying in the face of tradition if we reject the language of "winning" or "claiming" the world for Christ, but Jesus cried over Jerusalem precisely because it held its traditions too tightly, because it refused to listen to him as he criticized their usual ways of thinking — their traditional theology. He cried because he recognized that the few hosannas they would sing would be hollow praise. I'm sure that Jesus cries also over some traditional forms of arrogant witnessing that go on in his name yet today. When the Gospel that calls us to be self-giving and self-emptying channels of God's grace is converted into a Gospel that makes arrogant claims, then we have ceased to tell the true, original, old, old story of Jesus and his love. There is a huge difference between *proclaiming* the grace of God as seen in the stories of Jesus and *claiming* that anyone who doesn't accept a particular theology about Jesus is lost and damned. As the authors of *Bible and Mission* (Augsburg, 1986) point out: Mission is not "roping and branding" but loving, serving, learning, and forgiving.

Does all this talk of grace water down the Gospel to a message of cheap grace rather than free grace? Does it destroy the notion of the "saving work" of Christ? Of course not! Clearly there is nothing dainty or cheap about the grace shown to us on the Cross at Calvary. Hemmingway once defined courage as "grace under pressure" and theologian Paul Tillich saw Jesus as the embodiment of "the courage to be." To borrow Marshall McLuhan's expression, Jesus is both the medium and the message; his work and his message — his story — are one and the same thing.

So, to reject the image of soldiers in battle winning souls for the Lord is not to deny the importance of sharing the story of Jesus. A more gracious approach simply accents the positive and universal and inclusive message of the Gospel as over against the negative attitude expressed by the bumper sticker that says: "Read your Bible. It'll scare the hell out of you!"

Has the Christian message been watered down when a young Lutheran writes in a nationally published church journal of how he became "fired up" over a mission program to provide schools and classrooms in Africa? Not at all! Rather than cavalierly dismissing other faiths and cultures, we need to carry on an open dialogue with them in the name of Christian mission. Schools and classrooms are one good place to engage in such dialogue. Our appreciation of the scope of God's grace grows wonderfully when we look deeply into the insights of other religious traditions, when we encounter the Hindu concept of "salvation by the cat-hold" (the mother cat picking up the kitten by the nape of the neck is a symbol for unconditional acceptance), the Sikh veneration of the "True Name" as a way of showing that God is not limited by our particular names and ideas, the Zen "discovery" that enlightenment really comes only when we relax from our efforts and let it "happen to us!" Rather than rejecting dialogue or any form of worship with people who, as one Lutheran pronouncement recently said, "do not believe Christian faith-claims," let us welcome opportunities to better understand our religious/theological similarities and differences.

And let us enter into dialogue with good humor. The humility of humor, of not taking ourselves too seriously, is a much better model for Christian evangelism than the "winning" or "success" model! Martin Luther himself wrote that humor "is the true antidote to the sin of pride." Criticized for converting a tavern song into the hymn "A Mighty Fortress" Luther quipped: "Why should the devil have all the good tunes?" While preaching on the birth of Jesus, Luther questioned why the angels were flying around and singing instead of changing the baby's diapers. And, asked where God was before creation, Luther responded, "Making hell for the inquisitive."

The word "evangelical" is in grave danger of coming to mean simply "right wing" — in danger of becoming a political term. We must not let this happen. Better we should heed the words of Professor Timothy F. Lull, Lutheran Theological Seminary, Philadelphia: "The mission God has entrusted to us is a deep mystery. The question of how the church best may . . . perform that mission never can be finally or satisfactorily settled." (*Lutheran Standard*, March 20, 1987) The gospel is not about winners or losers or "final solutions." It is about being open channels of God's grace. It is about creativity, faith, hope and love.

Woody Hayes, the feisty Ohio State football coach, was eulogized by Richard Nixon as a man who "was never satisfied with success, and never discouraged by failure." Hayes himself made no apologies for his intensely competitive spirit. If never being satisfied with success, never being discouraged by failure, never apologizing for being competitive means that we hold values which go beyond winning, means that we always can see where there is room for improvement, then competition and success take their appropriate, limited place in our lives. We can even say that the Gospel story of Jesus is about love and goodness "winning out" over selfishness and evil. But an unbridled success/winner mentality is by definition selfish. In his olympics training, Brian Boitano was frequently reminded that being prepared to lose is just as important as training to win. All the world may love a gracious and giving winner. But no one loves a selfish winner. That is why the old, old story of Jesus constantly reminds us that abundant living is not about winning but is about loving, giving, and sharing.

Luke 13:1-9   Lent 3

Love Over Logic

Those eighteen upon whom the tower in Siloam fell and killed them, do you think they were worse offenders than all the others who dwelt in Jerusalem? I tell you, No.

(Luke 13:4-5a)

Reward and punishment! A basic fact of life! In San Francisco there is a chain of pastry stores called "Just Desserts" — a clever name with more than one level of meaning. "You've been good. Treat yourself! You deserve a reward." But many of us would also think: "Too many of these rewards and my just desserts will be obesity and poor health." The law of reward and punishment, of cause and effect, of action and consequences, is a pervasive part of our lives. Professionals who work with emotionally disturbed children often have to put a lot of effort into creating a structure of limits in which the child learns the connection between actions and consequences.

Many people also think of religion in terms of reward and punishment. One humorous quip in this vein says, "Work for the Lord, ... The pay isn't much but the retirement plan is out of this world!"

But our text from Luke today, like the story of the laborers in Matthew 20, who all received the same payment regardless of how long they had worked, is part of a consistent emphasis in the Gospels on a dimension that transcends the simple mathematics of reward and punishment. What we learn from this obscure event, where a tower fell on some people, says Jesus, is not that some sinners are worse than others and deserve more harsh punishment. That is not the point. What we learn is a lesson about God's patience with our failings. God is not in a hurry to pass final judgment on us. To borrow an image from modern psychology, God appears to have a "B-type personality," that is, God is more interested in encouraging us over and over again to be productive, positive, to be in the *process* of "bearing fruit," than in assessing the final, absolute, end result. (The A-type personality is preoccupied with the final goal while the B-type personality thinks more in terms of never-ending processes.) In Hindu-Buddhist theology the doctrine of Karma is sometimes thought of as a strict law of reward and punishment, but Karma can also be thought of as having to do more with a learning process in which the goal is *growth* — a kind of "end that never ends."

Many of the New Testament writers want us to see that the issues of life go much deeper than the limited logic of reward and punishment. Precisely because the Hebrew and Christian Scriptures put such a strong emphasis on doing justice, being righteous, and making the world into a lovely and wonderful place, the early Christian theologians realized that one of the deeper issues would be the danger of *despair* and dashed hopes among those who were making valiant efforts to "be perfect as your heavenly Father is perfect." The Christian faith is about doing the will of God: "Not those who say 'Lord, Lord,' but those who do the will of my Father will enter the kingdom of heaven." (Matthew 7:21) But, more precisely, the Christian message is about the *spirit in which* we go about our efforts to do good, to discover and do God's will, to make life beautiful. If we "do our best" in the spirit of trying to earn an eternal reward from God, we will realize in our moments of honesty that even our best, on those rare occasions when we may manage it, is not enough to make ourselves or our world perfect. We will be tempted either to lower our standards and expectations or to give in to despair and moral paralysis.

The Christian doctrine of sin is not an overly negative assessment of human nature. It is simply an honest recognition of the seemingly never ending tension between great expectations and tarnished realities. "The good that I would, I do not, and the evil that I would not, that I do." (Romans 7:19) In the face of such perplexity, such a predicament, talk of mere rewards and punishment according to our desserts — or of free-will versus determinism — seems shallow indeed.

Most people are not pathologically anti-social. Most of us want to do good, to do our best, to make life beautiful. The Bible, like other great writing, both secular and sacred, offers great insights into what it means to be ethical and good. But the Gospel that focuses on Jesus is primarily interested in the *attitude* we take toward our efforts to do "good works" and toward the fact that our "free wills" often appear to be in bondage to negative forces. And what is that attitude? There are any number of ways to describe it:

(1) We could call it the "Struggle and Relax" attitude. To borrow a phrase from army recruiters, God wants us to "be all that we can be." The spectre of unattainable rewards and the temptation to despair cannot be dissolved by simply lowering the standards of what we expect ourselves and the world to become — by giving up on "the Kingdom of God," by giving up on beauty. The problem is solved by paradoxically combining an attitude of struggle toward the best, with an attitude of relaxation that trusts God. Knowing in advance that even our best efforts are seldom if ever "good enough," we also know that God will not punish us for our failures because *God is more interested in having us keep on trying* than in having us reach some abstract goal of perfection. The "genius" of Christianity, if you will, is that it teaches us how to struggle and relax at the same time, how to continue hoping for the best even when it doesn't seem to be happening.

(2) One especially good way of describing the New Testament attitude toward our efforts to be and to do good, is to say that we learn from the Gospel how to combine *a sense of moral urgency* with *a sense of humor*! It is a seemingly impossible challenge to live by the spirit of the law rather than by the mere letter of the law. The challenge to love, pray for and understand our enemies — and even to be willing to "turn the other cheek" when the occasion calls for it — seems to require a virtually super-human amount of courage and good will. The vision of ourselves as part of God's plan to bring about the Kingdom of God on earth as it is in heaven seems grandiose and unrealistic. Yet the Christian Gospel speaks urgently of a Kingdom of God which is *at hand*! We are to take the Gospel of faith, hope and love with utmost seriousness. But how to do it without despairing? By combining our serious efforts with a profound sense of humor — with an overriding awareness of God's grace and forgiveness! Our sense of humor is a corollary to God's grace. A sense of humor — the ability not to take ourselves too seriously — is the opposite of a sense of urgency, but we must learn to combine these opposites in our attitude toward life. If we are too serious

and self-absorbed in our efforts to produce goodness, we tend to produce evil. (Stalin was very serious about creating his version of a better world.) If we are too lighthearted we will simply laugh off our problems and never really grapple with or solve any of them. We will begin habitually to use the phrase "I'm only human" as a cynical excuse.

When a usually very serious professor cracks a joke it is twice as funny because of the contrast with the professor's usual demeanor. This may well be the most profound observation about life that we can make: let us nurture the fine art of combining a radical sense of moral urgency with a radical sense of humor/grace. (Bishop Desmond Tutu seems to have mastered this art remarkably well.)

(3) Another great way to describe the Christian attitude toward "good works," toward moral and spiritual effort, is to remember the words of Saint Paul in 1 Corinthians 15:10: "I worked harder than any of them, though it was not I, but the grace of God which is with me." We would also do well to make a motto out of a line from Saint Ignatius Loyola, the founder of the Jesuit Order. He expressed this same profound paradox when he wrote: "Work hard and struggle as if everything depended on you; yet pray and trust God as if everything depended on God."

(4) Martin Luther once described *faith* as a good work! But he did not mean by it that "believing the right doctrines about Jesus" was the ultimate good thing we could do to save ourselves. Luther was fully aware that to speak of accepting Jesus by faith was a glorious contradiction — a paradox of grace. We automatically move beyond logic when we talk about "accepting Jesus," because the name Jesus itself *means* that *God accepts us*, that God alone is the cause of our salvation, of our reconciliation. By calling our faith in Jesus both a good work and a free gift from God, by emphasizing that God accepting us is more important than our accepting God, by recognizing that God's free will to save us is stronger than our free will to do what is evil or good, Luther was struggling to move us beyond the simple logic of earning reward and punishment to an awareness of the ultimate triumph of love and grace. He was struggling, as Saint Paul does in Romans 4, to re-interpret and/or develop our understanding of what grace and faith really mean. This is a part of what Jesus is talking about when he says in Luke 13:5 "Unless you repent, you will all likewise perish." Unless we

repent of the mindset that tries to *earn* God's acceptance and heavenly rewards, our efforts will indeed perish in despair.

"Were there no heaven to gain, no hell to flee; For what Thou art alone I must love Thee . . . not for the hope of glory or reward." (Spanish Hymn of unknown date)

Perhaps the biggest problem people have with a radical emphasis on the grace of God is that it seems to raise the controversial issue of "universalism," the question of whether a gracious God ultimately saves everyone. Quoting the old Spanish hymn where the poet says that he would love God even if there "were no hell to flee," I once preached a sermon on the ultimate redemptive power of God's grace. One parishioner later confronted me angrily: "If there's no hell, then there's no heaven!" Another complained to me that she refuses to believe that God could save or redeem, say, an Adolph Hitler. Dr. Walter F. Taylor, professor of New Testament studies at Trinity Seminary, Columbus, Ohio warned an evangelism conference in 1986 against "theories of universalism," and more than one church group has passed or attempted to pass resolutions condemning "the false doctrine of universalism."

The problem of universalism is also sometimes described as a matter of transforming "free grace" into "cheap grace." A theologian might argue that if God's grace is "too freely given" then the suffering and death of Jesus is belittled and cheapened. The average person might put it this way: "Why try to be a moral and good person if we're all going to the same place anyway?" In his article "Does Anyone Out There Care Anymore Whether People Believe in Jesus?", James Burtness attempts to show how the grace of God is *not totally free*: "Grace," he writes, "has been hammered at (people) in a manner so simplistic that they have become unable to distinguish between taking credit for their faith and taking responsibility for it." He feels that if we only take responsibility (not credit) for our salvation, then we have not compromised the emphasis on "salvation by grace alone." Coming at the issue from a different perspective, another theologian has written: "We can't choose *not* to be sinful, but we can choose to accept Jesus." Another standard way of trying to solve this dilemma is simply to say that if I am saved it is all God's doing and if I am lost it is all my own fault. Typically, this attempt to explain how grace is both totally free but at the same time not totally free, is combined with the observation that while God may *want* to save/redeem everyone, God is not *able* to do so because some folks are just beyond redemption. The Orthodox (Greek and Russian) churches frequently state their solution to the problem this way: "God does 99% of the work and humans do 1% of the work by accepting the gift of faith." Ultimately, however, all of these approaches and explanations deny the real paradox of grace and put the emphasis back on our own efforts to become right with God. (Classical Christian theology calls this the false doctrine of *synergism*.)

If the notion of universalism simply came out of the "humanistic doctrine" of the basic goodness and innocence of human nature, then one might easily reject it as naive and heretical. But when the radical New Testament emphasis on the grace of God is seen on its own terms as at least *tending* toward some form of universalistic thinking, then we realize that this issue is not easily ignored or settled. If the point is that people must "accept Christ" in order to be saved, are some people basically more sinful than others because they don't accept Christ? Or does God put more effort into saving those who do accept Christ? In either case, the radical idea of free grace, unconditionally given for all people, is compromised, and the unique message of Christianity evaporates. Neither is John Calvin's conclusion that God arbitrarily saves (elects) some people and not others a particularly good way of solving this problem. It puts arbitrariness over logic instead of love over logic.

To discuss the theological issue of universalism is to talk about what it means to go beyond the logic of eternal rewards and punishments. It is to ponder the paradox of a God who is both an absolutely just Judge and yet an absolutely gracious, forgiving Savior. The message of the New Testament is not that we should accept certain doctrinal propositions about Jesus or follow the "spiritual laws" leading to salvation, but that we should struggle in joyful hope with what it means to believe in the *radical grace of God!*

While the Unitarian Universalist Church believes unequivocally in universal salvation, we can be content to believe simply that universal salvation is *possible* when one considers the New Testament theme of the radical grace of God. I am content, in other words, to believe that it is not up to me to answer or decide this issue! Maybe God's final judgment will reveal that some people are indeed beyond redemption and will perish. Maybe it will reveal that the idea of "hell" is more than a picturesque image intended to shock us out of our ethical complacency and dullness. But let us learn what it means to say that such final judgment does indeed belong to God alone. You and I cannot pretend to know *who* is lost or saved. We can't even answer the prior question as to *whether* an ultimate separation of souls into the categories of "lost" and "saved" will in fact take place. We can only celebrate the Gospel message of the unconditional love and grace of God shown in Jesus, the Christ.

The Spanish poet had a great insight: We would learn much about the meaning of our faith if we would ask ourselves how important our religion would still be to us even *if* there were no heaven to gain or no hell to flee. (Would that the perpetrators of the Spanish Inquisition had asked themselves that question!) If we think that "being a good Christian" means giving up many pleasures now for the sake of heavenly pleasures later on, then we are likely to get angry even with this hypothetical question of "what if there were no heaven or hell?" We would want our self-denial rewarded and the self-indulgence of evil-doers punished. But if the values and notions of goodness proclaimed by the Gospel are valid, don't they have to be valid regardless of whether or not heaven is a part of the equation? If, as we have noted, Christian faith is about learning to live creatively in the dynamic tension between a sense of moral urgency and a sense of humor — if it is about learning to live in love — isn't it more than worthwhile to participate in such faith even if there were no "next life"? We must wonder about a person who is disgruntled with this world and can't wait for heaven. What makes us think we are going to be able to appreciate the next life if we have so little appreciation for the only life that we know about so far, namely, *this* life here and now? Christianity does not teach that we are put on this earth merely to earn a heavenly reward. We are here to celebrate life, love, creativity, faith and hope. We are here to celebrate what has been marvelously described as "the Eternal Now!"

Some don't care for her brand of comedy, but in her book, *Enter Talking*, Joan Rivers shares some profound insights. She writes: "The only way you can go into show business is to expect no reward at all . . . The paradox is: If you are *not* in it for the rewards, they are more likely to come to you . . . If you must go into the arts, go into them for yourself alone . . . be willing to paint a picture and just hang it on your wall." The Spanish poet expressed this same sentiment in his fifth stanza: "Not for the hope of glory or reward, But even as thou hast loved me Lord, I love thee . . ."

A young woman shocked everyone with her suicide attempt. She was an apparently successful, gifted person. In counseling she confided to her mother that her success had been motivated by an overpowering need to prove herself. She felt that she would only be loved if she competed and succeeded. *L. A. Law* star, Susan Dey, similarly reported in a *TV Guide* article that she was "petrified of everything — of not accomplishing enough, of not getting it right, of not being able to do it all." These three women are coming to realize that life is more about unconditional love than it is about success and rewards, that being loved and accepted just as we are *as people* must come first, with accomplishments a *distant* second.

At first it is hard to comprehend that Dr. Karl Menninger wrote both *The Crime of Punishment* and *Whatever Became of Sin?* The two books appear to be diametrically opposed. The one emphasizes that we must take Sin seriously while the other denounces the "philosophy of punishment" as obsolete, vengeful and itself *criminal*. But the two books are not contradictory. An emphasis on a gracious attitude of forgiveness, redemption and rehabilitation does not mean that we naively ignore sin and evil. Menninger writes that in place of the vengeful philosophy of punishment we should "seek a comprehensive, constructive social attitude — therapeutic in some instances, restraining in some instances, but preventative in its total social impact." He is calling for a paradoxical combination of judgment and grace.

To describe Christian evangelism as Channeling Grace is not to water down the Christian message to "cheap grace." It is not to ignore sin and evil. But it does imply a serious reproof of the attitude which objects even to the mere mention of the possibility of universal salvation out of a vengeful desire to see sinners punished. To describe Christian evangelism as Channeling Grace is to be aware of the ultimate *paradox* of judgement and grace. It is, simply, in the most profound sense, to value the positive over the negative, people over accomplishments, love over logic!

Luke 15:1-3, 11-32　　　　　　　　　　　　　　　　Lent 4

Save Us From the World-Savers

Now his elder son . . . was angry and refused to go in. His father came out and entreated him, but he answered his father. "Lo, these many years I have served you . . ."

(Luke 15:25a, 28-29a)

　　Garrison Keillor likes to describe his fictional town of Lake Wobegon, Minnesota, as having been founded by "Unitarian missionaries who came to convert the Indians through the use of interpretive dance." To appreciate the subtle humor of this remark we need to be aware that Unitarian Universalists generally don't believe in trying to convert people, and that while Unitarians do tend to favor "liturgical innovation," it seems likely that the Indians could have taught such missionaries more about dancing than the missionaries could have taught them. (It would have been like Don Rickles becoming a public relations agent to help Walter Cronkite improve his image.)

　　Today we tackle head-on the question of whether or not Christians are supposed to convert or save the world. Are we as members of the Christian church given the mission of "saving the heathen"? The simple answer is a resounding *No*! In fact, it is precisely the arrogant attitude of the self-appointed messiahs or holier-then-thou world-savers from which our faith in the name of Jesus saves us! Believing in Jesus *means* to believe that God alone can save us and the world. Pointing to God as the savior of the world serves, above all, to prevent us from being carried away with holier-than-thou delusions of grandeur.

　　The story of the Prodigal Son and his elder brother is one of many examples in the writings of Luke where the self-righteous are criticized, and the outcast or outsider is commended. It seems likely that the older brother in this parable was intended to represent a Judaism which condemned God's acceptance of the outsiders (the Gentiles), an acceptance proclaimed by Christianity. The prodigal son represents the Christian community and its identification with the poor, the needy, the outcast, the outsider, the Gentile. The irony is that today the situation may be reversed: Christians reject Jews and Judaism in both subtle and heavy-handed ways. When "Jews for Jesus" tells Jewish people that they can "accept Christ" and still remain Jewish, are they really respecting the integrity of Judaism, or are they actually trying to *trick* Jews into thinking that they can accept Christ without becoming Christians — without giving up Judaism as a faith commitment? We will come back to this question.

Most of us have probably asked or been asked at one time or another: "What about people who have never heard the Gospel?" The answer usually given to this question has two sides. One part of the answer is that we can only leave them in the hands of a gracious and just God. But the other part of the answer is troubling. It emphasizes how vital it is that we get busy spreading the Gospel. I say this is troubling because it tends to make us *compulsive* in our witnessing, and such compulsiveness easily becomes arrogance! We tend to slip into the attitude that it is up to *us* to save the world — that unless we convert people to Christ they will be lost and it will be *our fault*! The sad thing is that this compulsive, quilt motivated, won't-take-no-for-an-answer type of witnessing, actually turns people off to the Christian message by presenting a confusing and negative notion of what the Gospel is really about. Many people also have been turned off to almost any form of what they disparagingly call "organized religion," because it appears to be organized more for the sake of bringing people under its control than for the purpose of simply being an open channel of God's grace, flowing out freely, helping people to blossom and grow.

Charlie Liteky won a Congressional Medal of Honor during his service as a Roman Catholic chaplain in the Vietnam War. Eventually, however, he left the priesthood and in a first-of-its-kind ceremony, gave back his Medal. He has given up many of the comforts of life in order to become a crusader for peace. He almost starved himself to death in a 1986 protest against U. S. policy in Central America. On one occasion he said: "I am willing to die for our brothers and sisters in Nicaragua and El Salvador." He has also said that he needs to "help bring salvation to America." We can have great admiration for a person who sacrifices himself or herself for a great cause. But there comes a point when it is the person's ego that is at stake, not the salvation of the world. There is a thin line between self-sacrifice and self-serving delusions of grandeur.

A young woman named Barbara Underwood became rather visible in the media as a person who had been deprogrammed from the Moonies. She noted more than once that the most difficult thing about leaving the group was going from being a "world-saver" to being just one person among millions. But she had come to realize the many pitfalls of the "world-saver" mentality. You begin to arrogantly believe that you have all the answers. You refuse to really listen to anyone else's point of view because you are sure it is "from the devil." You will use any questionable tactic or clever manipulation to further your cause. The list goes on and on. Barbara Underwood was grateful that she had been saved from the compulsion to save the world. How much better it is to trust God with that ultimate goal!

Writing in his congregational newsletter, Pastor Walter Werronen of San Rafael, California observed: "In evangelism work God really cannot use those who have an incurable desire for personal glory . . . This is why God chose people who were so insignificant that they could have no natural cause for boasting." We must extend this insight even to cover those who think that by "claiming the world for Christ" they are merely being humble servants of a Christ-centered theology. When we act as if it is up to *us* to save the world by *our* witnessing, *our* theology, *our* service, then we are being "Christ-centered" in the wrong way. To be truly Christ-centered is to remember what it means to say that "Jesus is the name above every name." It means to believe that God is the only "world-saver" and that we must never usurp that role! It is not enough to eschew our personal glory. We must also beware of that subtle *extension* of personal glory which masquerades as humble witnessing.

Christian evangelism all too easily deteriorates into the *selling* of a system of answers, a particular, narrowly defined lifestyle or a particular notion of "civilization." The stories which show Jesus affirming outcasts of various kinds are what the Christian Gospel is really about. This story of the Prodigal Son, the parable of the Good Samaritan, the story in the book of Acts where Phillip baptizes the Ethiopian eunuch (Acts is clearly from the same pen as Luke) — all of these are part of Luke's theme of God's love for the poor, the minority, the oppressed, the outsider, the needy, the sinner! While the motif of God's identification with all people in their struggles — their suffering, their growing pains, their neediness — is present throughout the New Testament, this way of stressing God's grace is particularly evident in the Luke/Acts writings.

Twice in her autobiography, Joan Rivers explains why she and other outrageous humorists seem to be particularly popular with gay audiences. She says that gays are like Jews and like many comedians — victims, outcasts, born into trouble, living in trouble, not accepted. "When you are an outsider, hungry for recognition, you can be noticed by being outrageous and the more you ridicule your pain, the less it hurts — and that is why I love gays; they will go far out with me into silliness." Like many eunuchs in those days, the one baptized by Phillip *may* have been gay. If we remember this, it will help to prevent us from letting Christianity deteriorate into nothing more than the promotion of a provincial, cultural model or lifestyle. H. Richard Niebuhr's famous book *Christ and Culture* also helps to make it clear that we must not simply assume that the Christian faith is either for or against a particular culture or lifestyle. Niebuhr makes it clear that to be a part of the Christian movement is to be engaged in constant dialogue and struggle with the particular society or culture in which we find ourselves. To be a follower of Jesus is to be involved in the ethical tension between our desire for moral absolutes and the reality of ethical relativity. Instead of pretending to have all the answers about life we can laugh along with the joke that says: "In these complex and confusing times, if you're not confused, you don't understand the situation!"

"Lost in the night do the people yet languish . . . Light o'er the land of the needy is beaming . . ." (Finnish Song)

In another of his newsletter articles, pastor Walt Werronen tells of a graduate theology student friend of his who "does not approve of preaching to the heathen. He would prefer to be a missionary who goes to affirm the religious experiences of the people of the country and have respect for their ethnicity and religious heritage." While identifying himself as a member of an older generation, Pastor Werronen affirms the need for new ways of conceiving and doing evangelism. He would seem to be sympathetic with the newer translation of one of his homeland's most famous hymns which substitutes the word "needy" for the word "heathen." The hymn is called "Lost in the Night" and the last stanza begins: "Light o'er the land of the *needy* is beaming." The call for a new approach to evangelism does not mean that Christians should go to the extreme of not even inviting people to church services, as if to do so would be to infringe upon their freedom. It is not arrogant for us as Christians to share the message of the New Testament Gospel and its interpretation of Jesus as God's anointed one, the Messiah, the Christ. Pointing out our common human neediness is not arrogant or boastful.

What we must learn to do is to share the unique message of the Christian faith without implicitly or explicitly conveying the arrogant attitude which says "Christianity is the one, true, best religion." In other words, we must learn to be Jesus-centered in the right way. A 1987 article in *The Lutheran* magazine clearly shows a sensitivity to the danger of the world-saver syndrome, as it reports on six goals for a model evangelism program. The first two stated goals are to improve and strengthen the overall *morale* of pastors and congregations. The third goal is to deepen the spiritual life of those within the Christian community. The fourth is simply to affirm the responsibility of the individual for sharing faith while the fifth speaks of creating an attractive climate of growth within congregations. The sixth goal stresses the development of inclusive visions of what the Christian community should be, not just racial inclusiveness but inclusiveness in terms of such things as economic status and lifestyles as well.

The significant thing to notice about these goals is that they focus on making our faith come alive *for ourselves* rather than on how we can "convert the heathen." God's grace is more likely to flow through us to others if we relax in our faith and avoid the world-saver image! The Prodigal's older brother may have been a good and obedient son. But he took himself too seriously! He was too enamored with his own righteousness to be able to see and appreciate the larger righteousness and goodness of his loving father. We behave like him when we act as if it is up to us to save the world with our religious, political or social agenda — as if we know better than God how it must be done. We become dangerous fanatics if we do not balance the "God-has-no-hands-but-our-hands" idea with the equally valid point that "God has the whole world in His hands." To believe in God is, in part, precisely the same thing as refusing to take ourselves too seriously!

Another important aspect of our realization that it is not up to us to save or convert the world, is that it clarifies the attitude that we who are Christians should take toward Judaism and the other world religions. Since our belief in Jesus means that we trust God alone to handle the matter of every person's eternal destiny, therefore, we cannot put limits on who God can save! We do not need to worry that God can't save Jews unless they give up their Judaism, or Buddhists unless they give up their Buddhism. We can enjoy open dialogue with all people and all faiths without the hidden agenda that desperately needs to convert everyone. At a symposium on "Jews and Christians in Dialogue," Episcopal theologian Paul van Buren and Paulist priest Michael McGarry called on the church to develop a theology of why we don't convert Jews, and noted that the Jewish people are an enduring sign of God's faithfulness.

Sad to say, it may well be that one aspect of anti-Semitism is the overt or subliminal feeling on the part of some Christian people that since Jews so stubbornly refuse to "accept Christ" they must be somehow less than fully human and can, therefore, be treated accordingly. It goes back to the old mistake of thinking that the New Testament condemns "the Jews" when, in fact, what the Gospel of Jesus really condemns is self-righteousness — the kind of arrogant self-righteousness that dares to make ultimate judgments about another person's worth in the eyes of humanity and God. We should shudder to consider what a short step it is from the world-saver mentality to the "final-solution" mentality of Hitler's Third Reich.

Elie Wiesel, prophetic survivor of Nazi death camps, won the Nobel Peace Prize in 1986. If ever there was a man whose message might save the world, he is one of them. Yet he is incredibly humble. A San Francisco *Chronicle* editorial said of him: "There is no visible ego in the man . . . he does not profess to have all the answers . . . he dwells not on our actions of the past but our responsibility for the future . . . he has become an advocate for life, peace and human dignity."

God save us from self-appointed world-savers! Such Messiah-complexes look shallow and dangerous next to a person like Wiesel. Meeting Elie Wiesel reminds one of the New Testament image of Jesus as reluctant to be identified as Messiah or Christ. The world is not saved by people who blow their own horns.

John 12:1-8   *Lent 5 (Common)*

Love Is Down to Earth

The poor you always have with you, but you do not always have me.

(John 12:8)

    Like me, I suppose, you have probably wondered about the popularity of such TV shows as "Lifestyles of the Rich and Famous," "Dallas," and "Dynasty." It would seem that our value systems have become much too materialistic. One wonders if any really serious attempts are being made to close the gap between the rich and the poor. It has been observed that even "socialists" who seem to be interested in the welfare of poor people do not really so much love the poor; it is, rather, that they hate the rich!

    Our story here is from John rather than Luke. When John's Gospel shows us Jesus telling his disciples "the poor you always have with you," are we seeing a Jesus who is less sympathetic to the poor and oppressed than the Jesus we see in Luke? Does Luke virtually hate the rich, the comfortable, the establishment . . . and does John correct this imbalance by showing Jesus willing to indulge in a little luxury, willing to put his concern for the poor on hold and attend to a socially approved custom? Some commentators have expressed shock at this apparent callousness on the part of Jesus toward the poor. Does Jesus, at least as John sees him, believe that poverty and suffering are inevitable and that efforts to eliminate it are hopeless? (The Buddhist-styled group called *Eckankar* does teach that it is a sinful waste of time to try to reform this world because only the next world matters.)

    When Jesus says that we will not always have him with us as we will always have the poor, we might conclude that Jesus is indulging in some unseemly self-congratulation, that he is setting himself off from, above, and over against the poor. It is true that by the time the Gospel of John was written in the form that we have it today, the early church had developed a much stronger conviction of Jesus as a triumphant victor over sin and death, but this was nothing like the naive theology of glory "for winners only" that we have been warning ourselves against.

The absolutely essential thing to notice is that even in John's exalted images of Jesus as the Good Shepherd, The Resurrection and the Life, The Truth, etc., *Jesus himself never stops being one of the poor!* Jesus is not saying "forget the poor and pay attention to me." He is saying, rather, "quit talking about 'the poor' in general and pay attention to the specific poor, needy person right in front of you!" Just as the philosophers Immanuel Kant and Martin Buber have insisted that we must treat people as ends in themselves rather than as simply means to end, so Jesus is pictured by John as wanting to be treated as an end in himself and not just as a means to an end. Jesus is not just a symbol of the poor and oppressed; he is himself specifically "stricken, smitten and afflicted."

The musical *Hair* has within it a most provocative song called "Easy To Be Hard." The gist of the song is that it is easy to "care about the bleeding crowd" while yet totally ignoring "a needy friend." A little joke you may have heard makes the same point: "I love mankind . . . it's people I can't stand!" Jesus does not set himself apart from the poor. He simply points out that he himself, as one of the specific poor, has needs — and that Mary has been sensitive to those needs. By contrast, Judas pretends to be concerned for the poor (in general) but is actually only concerned about himself.

We must also be sure to notice that Jesus relates the costly ointment not to his own personal glorification but to his *burial.* To the degree that this "luxury" is a symbol, it is a symbol of his humble self-sacrifice unto death. Even more than his humble birth, Jesus' death on the Cross is the ultimate expression of his identification with the poor and lowly!

In his thoughtful, questioning lyrics for the musical *Jesus Christ, Superstar,* Tim Rice gives this slant to the words of Jesus: "Surely you're not saying we have the resources to save the poor from their lot? . . . Think! while you still have me. Move! while you still see me." The suggestion is that in the larger scheme of things we have to set priorities and sometimes that means putting a specific need above a general problem. For example, we do need to put resources into political and economic efforts to change and improve the *system* whereby we distribute the world's wealth. We can and should engage in political advocacy on behalf of justice. But there are also times when specific, emergency relief is needed in a crisis. According to Tim Rice, Jesus is saying in this story that this special moment in time, this "kairos moment" (as the Greeks would call it), must take precedence over the long-term general concern for the welfare of all poor, oppressed and lowly people. Jesus is in crisis and it is time to get down to brass tacks!

"The cup of water given for you still holds the freshness of your grace." (Frank M. North)

In fact, this metaphor of getting down to brass tacks expresses one of the most important features of biblical theology. In many ways, the Bible is an extremely down-to-earth book. Most specifically, it is about *love coming down to earth*. The Christmas story is the story of God's love come down to earth. It is the story of Emmanuel — God with us. It is the story of "incarnation," God in the flesh! God is indeed involved where the rubber hits the road. Martin Luther put it somewhat differently when he said, "God is interested in a lot of things besides religion." Whatever is done for "the least of these" is done for God. "The cup of water given for you still holds the freshness of your grace."

One facet of this down-to-earth character of the Bible is the earthy tone of many incidents described. The biblical writers are quite matter-of-fact about describing sexual matters and bodily functions. Some contemporary authors like James Nelson in *Embodiment* (Augsburg) and Larry Uhrig in *Sexual Ethics* (Alyson Publications) show how this honest earthiness could help us replace overly "sex-negative" attitudes with "sex-positive" attitudes. In an over-zealous concern to warn about the dangers of misused sexuality, many people develop a basically sex-negative outlook which is not in keeping with the biblical concept of the goodness of creation. In the story of Lazarus, John is not squeamish about mentioning the stink of a man dead four days (John 11:39), and Luke tells us in Acts chapter 8 of the eunuch, a person considered by many to be a sexual outcast, who becomes one of the important converts to Christianity. Christian love is truly down-to-earth!

Another facet of the Bible's down-to-earthness is evident precisely in its concern for the poor. Overall, the biblical writers are not anti-materialistic. They are critical only of the wrong kind of materialism — *selfish* materialism. Earthly goods are not to be ignored or destroyed. They are to be *shared*! Pete Seeger, the folksinger, has said that "share" is a better word than "love." He has a point. We also fall prey to the wrong kind of materialism if we adopt "success" as a model for the New Testament Gospel. Too often the oversimplified message goes out that "spiritual success" will lead to material success, when in fact the Gospel of Jesus promises neither forms of "success." We can agree with the pundit who has dubbed such "success gospels" as "mindless, shallow, *consumerist* approaches to Christianity."

Jesus' reference to the poor who are always with us reminds us of his other specific references to the poor, particularly in the Beatitudes: "Blessed are the poor" (as Luke has it) or "the poor in spirit" (as in Matthew), "for theirs is the Kingdom of heaven." While it is likely that Luke's version refers to the down-to-earth poverty of the poor, it is possible that, like Matthew's version, it also refers to the blessedness of those whose piety is *simple*. As noted in the Ash Wednesday sermon, the New Testament celebrates "the piety that isn't." True piety is a simple piety that will spend at least as much money on feeding the hungry, for example, as on promoting television shows. One critic referred to "Moral Sloberts" as his way of satirizing the self-agrandizing form of so-called evangelism. When Oral Roberts was saying that the Lord would "call him home" if he didn't raise eight million dollars, a black minister appearing on the Oprah Winfrey Show provided perhaps the best and most insightful response. He said that it seemed somewhat presumptious to reduce God's purview to concern over *a mere eight million dollars*! God does have ways of calling us back to simple piety, of calling us back down to earth!

In the upcoming series of Easter sermons we will meet quite a number of times the theme of Jesus' words in this text: "you do not always have me." The church and the Scriptures have developed a number of ways of describing how Jesus remains present with us here on earth even though physically he obviously is "no longer with us." One of these ways of explaining how Jesus is in a sense still concretely with us is the concept of the "apostolic succession." In some churches this is taken to mean that there is an unbroken line of succession and ordination directly from Jesus through the apostles to the priesthood of the church today. In others, "apostolic succession" is seen as referring more simply to the unbroken tradition of the authentic teaching of the Gospel by anyone who truly teaches it. The ecumenical debate between those who stress the authority of the ordained clergy as literal successors of Jesus and those who stress the "spiritual" succession of the "true preaching and teaching of the Gospel" is one of the major roadblocks to formal Christian unity today. Perhaps if both sides will be more humble and recognize the dangers of yelling too stridently about who represents the true church, we will all remain true to the simple piety that Jesus referred to when he said "Blessed are the poor in spirit."

Finally, let us ask what down-to-earth evangelism should be all about. Some would insist that it means concrete concern for adding numbers of people to membership rolls. But it should ever be our conscious goal. It is likely that people can tell whether we are really interested in their needs and concerns or whether we are simply after "members." We are called not to pursue growth for growth's sake, but as Pastor Timothy Wright of Glendale, Arizona has written, to speak only in terms of "growth for the sake of others." Just as happiness comes as a by-product of a meaningful life rather than as the result of a conscious "pursuit of happiness," so organizations including the church, grow as a by-product of real concern for people. A recent *People* magazine article told of sister Anne Brooks, a doctor and nun, who "practices without preaching to the poor in a battered Mississippi delta town." Significantly, she is a member of the Sisters of the Holy Names of Jesus and Mary, and she clearly understands what the name *Jesus* means. Her humility is awe-inspiring. She says: "I'm not here to make anybody Catholic. The faith of these people is deeper than my own . . . This place has changed me so much. I'm less selfish . . . I've learned not to expect instant results . . . because you learn from poor people how to wait . . . I receive much more from these people than I could ever give them."

The Reverend Cathy Hagstrom George has written of her work in women's prisons in Massachusetts: "Jesus became one of the despised and rejected of his society, and it is among these (poor and despised people) that his words and teaching have the most power. In all of his dealings with people, one fundamental change transpires . . . their dignity is restored . . . he restores the value and worth of the person in whatever way it was missing . . . I have come to know criminals who are first and foremost *victims* — victims of poverty, addiction, sexism, racism, abuse and violence . . . The moral reality of the Christian message is that we are all, in the eyes of God, equally needy and equally deserving of God's tender mercy . . . My teachers have been women I have come to know and love, despair and grieve over. Through them I have been made aware of the powerful presence of God in those who suffer yet still hope."

Here we glimpse what it means to say that the love of Jesus is truly down-to-earth, even if we don't literally have him with us. Lent is a time to contemplate the many poets who have asked "Where is Christ being sacrificed now?", a time to see how we are all in need of God's grace, a time to look for down-to-earth ways of sharing God's love.

Luke 20:9-19 (L)   *Lent 5 (Lutheran)*

Jesus, Mary, Gustav Mahler, Brother Martin, and the Magi

The scribes and the chief priests . . . perceived that he had told this parable against them.

(Luke 20:19)

    No doubt you are wondering what Jesus, his mother, Mary, the composer, Gustav Mahler, Martin Luther and the three Wise Men (the Magi) have in common. The list sounds like it comes from one of Johnny Carson's "Carnak" bits, doesn't it? The simple answer is that all of these people were willing to take a new look at the traditions they had inherited. Like Tevye in *Fiddler On The Roof*, they could celebrate the glory of *tradition*! But, like him, they also realized that tradition must remain in dialogue with a changing world.

    Pinchas Peli is a modern rabbi-turned-teacher who likes to say "I don't come to preach — I come just to think along with you." In his book, *Torah Today*, published in 1987, he displays his special gift for blending tradition with new ideas and insights. He says that people who see no reason to be in touch with their religious traditions are like people who say "I've listened to enough concerts, I've read enough books, I quit." Then he adds: "There are concerts, books waiting. Why deprive yourself?" Peli reminds us that the Jewish Talmud encourages and welcomes differing opinions. It assumes that we will do new thinking on old issues but that we will always check these new ideas and new issues against a tradition that is more than 3000 years old. It has been said that if progressive John XXIII had been Pope at the time of Martin Luther there would still be a unified church under the papacy, and "St. Martin of Germany" would be known today as the founder of the Lutheran Order.

Perhaps, too, if there had been more leaders like Rabbi Peli at the time of Jesus, the Christian interpretation of what the "Messiah" was all about would have been better understood.

Let us think along together about this parable of the tenants who thought that they could usurp the prerogatives of the owner of their land. They thought that they were "set" in their position and didn't have to listen to any new messages from the owner. Clearly, they represent the Jewish leaders who in the name of their tradition refused to listen to prophets and to Jesus when they came with new and challenging messages. In the Gospel of Matthew this criticism of the "lawyers and Pharisees" is stated in its strongest terms. Stephen Schwartz paraphrased these famous "woes!" in his musical *Godspell* like this: "Alas for you, lawyers and Pharisees, Hypocrites that you be . . . Sure that the kingdom of heaven awaits you . . . I send you prophets and I send you preachers, Sages in rages and ages of teachers, Nothing can mar your mood. Hypocrites . . . who murdered the prophets . . . Blind guides! Blind fools!" Now it needs to be said as strongly as possible in this post-Holocaust world that these kinds of strong condemnations are not directed ultimately at any one, specific group of people! This is a condemnation of all hypocrisy, of all arrogant traditions, religious or otherwise, that blindly destroy anything that criticizes or challenges their established notions and authority. To put it another way, there is an anti-establishment theme in the Gospels (especially in Luke), along with the theme of sympathy for the outsider, the outcast and the poor. Somewhat ironically, today we must take note of Rabbi Peli's observation that the vast majority of Jews have always known what it means to be the "eternal outsider." Anyone can become the outsider with whom God symphathizes, and anyone can slip into being the hypocritical oppressor who rejects God in the very act of claiming to uphold God's will and law.

We Christians, too, can fall into this trap of being traditionbound. When Lutherans, especially, celebrate their heritage as a *reformation* movement, they should remind us all of the danger of holding our traditions too tightly.

"Jesus . . . may our eyes be ever turning to behold your cross anew."
(Savonarola)

Reformers like Girolamo Savonarola, who admonishes us in his hymn "Jesus, Refuge of the Weary" to be always willing to take a new look at the Cross, and Martin Luther, who was declared an outlaw for his new vision of the old traditions, stand in a long tradition (!) of seers who took a new look at an ancient faith. The "Wise Men" or "Three Kings" in Matthew 2 are actually more specifically identified in the Greek as "Magi." That is, they were priests of the Zoroastrian faith, the ancient Persian religion. That these leaders of another religious tradition were willing to take an open-minded look at a new and perhaps different faith is cause for us designating them as especially wise. (We must also note here that the Persian/Zoroastrian king Cyrus is described in the book of Isaiah as "God's anointed" — God's Messiah! — when he allows the Jews to return home from captivity in Babylon.) The point is that the Bible celebrates people who are open to new ideas, open to new visions of ancient traditions, open to the unpredictable ways of God.

The philosopher Frederich Nietzsche's vision of the relationship between Christianity and Zoroastrianism embodied a bold criticism of the Christian faith, a critique later adopted by Malcolm X and others. Nietzsche took Zoroaster's name — his famous book is called *Thus Spake Zarathustra* (same name, different version) — as the symbol of a religion for the strong, as over against Jesus whom he saw as promoting a religion of weakness. Nietzsche wanted a religious figure who would stand for strength, self-reliance and assertiveness, in contrast to the emphasis Jesus put upon mercy, love and "turning the other cheek." Of course, the philosophy of the "superhuman," or "superman," that he developed apparently fails to understand that it takes strength to love and to forgive, but Nietzsche's ideas *have* stimulated some creative thinking. Malcolm X forced a lot of us to ask if we might not be using "a lily-white Jesus" to oppress people of non-European races and cultures, and he hoped that Muhammad might better symbolize black independence. The great composer Gustav Mahler was an adherent of Nietzsche, and not "typically devout," but he was deeply spiritual in his own way. His great "Resurrection Symphony No. 2" is one of the great contemporary statements of the Christian theme of resurrection. It would be impossible to calculate how many people have been inspired by this amazing piece of music.

Nietzsche's virtually irreligious notion of self-reliance seems to fly in the face of the Christian message of reliance upon the grace of God, but on one level at least, these opposite concepts lead to a similar attitude. Out of traditional Christian reliance upon the grace of God, comes the seemingly nontraditional concept of "religionless Christianity." To rely totally upon the grace of God is tantamount to affirming that ultimate "religious" concerns like my eternal destiny are so much in God's hands that I can in a sense forget about such matters and concentrate my attention on the here-and-now. I can, so to speak, thank God that I am freed from "religious worries" to relax and concentrate on taking responsibility for this world that we have been given! Paradoxically, Nietzsche's doctrine of self-reliance and the Christian doctrine of reliance upon the grace of God converge to produce what might quite appropriately be called *"religious* secular humanism!"

I realize that upon hearing of such non-traditional, paradoxical notions as "religionless Christianity" and "religious/secular humanism," some Christians may have a first impulse to kill or quash the bearer of such a message. But before we jump to the conclusion that this kind of thinking denies our tradition, we should refer ourselves to this parable that Luke directs at the religious leaders who rejected the prophetic voice. The Bible, the Talmud, the Mishnah, the history of Christian doctrine — all reflect an ongoing process of reinterpreting tradition. The reinterpretation of tradition is not necessarily a denial of that tradition.

As the Magi were wise enough to be open to a new and tradition-challenging message, so Christians in turn need to be open to the insights of other religious traditions. In an article titled "Private gain and public good in the American Dream," Ronald Thiemann, Dean of Harvard Divinity School, wrote: "Genuine religious pluralism means that Christians, as well as others, must recognize themselves as one religious voice among many in the public conversation . . . we must restrain those forces that seek to impose some form of Christian politics on American public life." Then he added, "I am convinced that the mainstream religious communities will recover their public voices only when they seek to appropriate and reform their own religious traditions . . . we must develop a new vision of how excellence and compassion, self-interest and virtue, private gain and public good can once again be brought together."

One of the things we can learn from the voice of Hinduism is that there are different *styles* of being religious. Hindus distinguish between what they call the way of devotion, the way of ritual, and the way of knowledge. In other words, we will understand one another better if we simply accept the fact that there are different "religious personality types." Some people are by nature devotional and pious — they express their faith in very warm, emotional terms, as if "the Lord" is always visible right at their elbow. Other folk express their faith primarily through forms and rituals. And still others tend to be intellectualizers; they might even say of themselves that they are "not religious" when what they mean is that their piety does not take the more typical form of devotion or ritual. We need to learn that God's grace can be channeled through all of these religious styles.

Another religious voice that too often has not been heard is that of women. In recent years a significant number of Christians have taken to clown imagery as a way of expressing their faith, and Dr. Marge Wold, who worked for years as a Director of Ministry in Changing Communities for a major denomination, expounded on that new tradition in a series of lectures in 1985 titled "Clowns, prophets, chaos: hope for the city." Listen to these samples of her way of looking anew at the Cross: "Ministry in the city requires the qualities of a clown and the plot of a comedy. We need the kind of humor that winks at our audacity in entering such a complex sociological system at all with a 2000-year-old rural paradigm about shepherds and lost sheep." Speaking of what it means to be a prophet, she emphasized how difficult it is for a clergyperson/pastor to be the tradition-shaking prophet, and encouraged clergy to support the laity in the prophetic "creative process, and the apparent chaos which is an integral and essential part of it." Dr. Wold laments that "although the people of our churches have been exposed to persons from different backgrounds, worldviews, and cultural value systems through contacts in the work place, in our neighborhoods, in schools and through the mass media, little of this awareness has impacted congregational practices. Any deviation from traditional patterns of behavior, instead of being seen as an opportunity for growth and enrichment of congregational life, is feared as a mark of decay and dissolution." She concludes, "John's vision of the, 'great multitude which no one could number, from every nation, from all tribes and peoples and tongues' tells us what we are about in a pluralistic society."

Marge Wold understands that it is indeed *traditional* for the Christian faith to be open to diversity! Have we been guilty of *defining people out of the church* by a too-narrow view of what constitutes an appropriate Christian lifestyle or value system? A recent survey of the San Francisco Bay Area indicated that only about 3% attend worship regularly. Is this because sophisticated city people are simply irreligious, or is it because Christians are allowing the church to be ghettoized by small-minded notions of what the Christian community stands for? If people are to be "tripped up" by the church, let us be sure that they stumble over Christ — over the "foolishness" of God's vulnerable and unconditional love — and not over some parochial, culturally-limited version of Christianity.

The religious leaders in our text tripped over Jesus, not realizing that he was the cornerstone of something new that God was making with their tradition. Perhaps a modern parallel is to be found in an open letter written to Pope John Paul II by a group of gay church people before his visit to San Franaisco: "Your predecessors condemned Galileo when he said the earth revolved around the sun. Your clergy claimed Galileo was sinful in stating this scientific fact. You have the right to your own beliefs, however incorrect they may be, but you do not have the right to interfere with our lives on the basis of those beliefs." The signatories of this letter were objecting to the Vatican's condemnation of homosexuality. As Christians they were rightly reminding the church of how often in the past, by rejecting what is new, challenging or threatening — by shrinking from the struggle with controversial issues — we have been rejecting the truth and refusing to grow! Even the reform-minded Martin Luther rejected the concepts of Galileo and Copernicus.

Actually, you know, at the very beginning of his Gospel, Luke calls our attention to a young woman named Mary, whose attitude sets the stage for the entire ministry and message of Jesus. We should always remember and ponder her words as we move through our lives: "(God) has put down the mighty from their thrones, and exalted those of low degree." We might also paraphrase and say: God sometimes puts aside or modifies our traditions, and breaks into our lives with good tidings of great joy — giving us an exciting new outlook on life!

John 8:1-11 (RC)	Lent 5 (Roman Catholic)

Some Women's Stories

Let him who is without sin among you be the first to throw a stone at her.

(John 8:7)

    This story of the woman caught in adultery might be described as a "second-class story" — because it seems to have been added to John's Gospel as an afterthought. It does not appear in any of the older and more original versions of John, and some experts on the New Testament even think it may belong in Luke. The second-class status of this story is, unfortunately, also mildly appropriate . . . in light of the fact that throughout history, women have been accorded second-class recognition in most societies. In recent years we have all been more or less in the throes of revising — of "revisioning" — our male-dominated, patriarchal society. Women have probably always had more strength and influence than men would like to admit, but today fewer and fewer women are content to live with limited notions of a woman's role and place in society.

    One of the reasons it is appropriate to associate this story with *Luke's* Gospel, is that along with his concern for outcasts, for the poor and oppressed, Luke also displays perhaps a greater empathy and respect for women than any other writer/editor in the New Testament. Beginning with the provocative story of Mary, who is proclaimed as a prime example of how God exalts those "of low degree," of how God is exceedingly concerned to rescue people from second-class status, Luke pays a lot of attention to women: the prophetess, Anna; the daughter of Jairus; the widow who gave her last mite to help others — these and other women we meet nowhere else, except in Luke. But John also credits Jesus' mother with propelling Jesus into his ministry at the wedding in Cana, and in Chapter

4 he explicitly makes a point of how the disciples of Jesus "marveled that he was talking with a woman" so seriously. It seems clear that, in general, the Gospel writers were ahead of their time in taking women seriously! Both the Samaritan woman at the well and the disciples are surprised when Jesus talks with her because, as is still the case with Orthodox Jews today, strict custom separated men and women in certain ways. It was considered inappropriate for Jesus to talk with a lone woman in such an informal setting — especially an outcast Samaritan woman! It is not at all far-fetched to see Jesus as a forerunner of both women's and men's liberation movements. He was willing to cross artificial barriers and challenge customary sex roles. In this story of the woman at the well, Jesus explains and demonstrates by his actions that those who worship "in spirit and in truth" may find themselves protesting social customs — like the establishment of male dominance — in the name of higher principles.

But the story of the woman caught in adultery from our main text here in John 8 is not just a woman's story. It is a story that reinforces a consistent theme in John's Gospel, the theme stated most eloquently in the famous John 3:16-17 passage: "God so loved the world . . . God sent not his son into the world to condemn the world." This story calls into question any type of condemning and judging attitudes that label other people as outcasts. God did not send his son into the world to create outcasts and outsiders, but to celebrate the unity and diversity of many sheepfolds, many mansions. The point of this story is that Jesus is critical only of those who self-righteously condemn others. He says, "Let him who is without sin among you be the first to cast a stone at her." (A more contemporary version of this saying would be: "People who live in glass houses shouldn't throw stones.") The smug self-righteousness of those who were about to stone this woman to death does become an issue of sexism, if we assume that it was men who were so eager to kill her while apparently not being equally eager to stone the male partner in the alleged adultery situation. Be that as it may, the fundamental point remains simply that Jesus is warning against "holier-than-thouism" in all its forms. He is questioning our right to turn anyone into an outcast, an outsider, a second-class member of the human race.

A joke has been told about this story, that when Jesus said "Let anyone who is without sin cast the first stone at her," there was a sudden silence; but then all at once a huge boulder slammed down on the woman, and Jesus turned behind him and said, "Mother! *Really*!" The assumption is that Jesus' mother, Mary, was immaculately conceived and hence sinless, so she could throw a stone; but if Jesus himself doesn't condemn the woman, why should Mary do so? If even God's ultimate power to judge is always tempered with mercy, how much more should we beware of a condemning attitude! Certainly we can admonish people on the basis of ethical principles, and we can resist and restrain harmful actions, but it is never *our* prerogative to condemn, to expel a person from the human race, to label anyone as beyond God's love.

We have to realize that our ethical principles and evaluations are not flawless. The church is right to stand up for the traditional ethic of marital fidelity. But conservers of tradition also have to deal with the fact that circumstances alter cases. Strict ethical standards must stand in tension with the old Native American saying that one should not criticize others if one has not walked a mile in their moccasins. Take, for example, the stories of two fairly young women. Both have husbands who have been severely injured and who require permanent nursing home placement. The one wife decides eventually to divorce her husband and marry another man. She continues to care for her former husband, but knows she cannot survive without the multi-dimensional love and intimacy that her new husband can provide. The other wife remains married to her invalid husband, but she develops an intimate relationship with another man whose wife is also in permanent nursing home care. I think Jesus would tell us not to judge or condemn either of these women on the basis of some general principle. We have not walked in their shoes.

We do not know the total situation of the woman accused of adultery in the presence of Jesus. Perhaps Jesus did know. When he told her to go her way and sin no more he was not necessarily condemning what she had done to get in the fix she was in. The author of the story may be thinking of Jesus as being aware of extenuating circumstances. (The Gospel of John does have a rather lofty notion of Jesus' God-like special powers.) But regardless of all that, the admonition to "sin no more" is simply Jesus' way of giving the woman another chance. The whole point of the New Testament emphasis on forgiveness in not to focus on past sins but continually to remind ourselves that tomorrow is another day, that God always offers us a new opportunity to improve, to do good, to love rather than to condemn.

At the cross her station keeping, stood the mournful mother weeping, close to Jesus to the last. (13th Century Liturgical Composite)

Not long ago a woman who had been brutally raped and blinded came on the Sally Jessy Raphael TV talk show to share her experiences. She made a remarkable witness to the way in which she deals with her anger toward the man who so irreparably damaged her life. She said, "He has already taken too much of my time and energy; I'm not going to waste any more of my life by focusing on him." At the Cross, Jesus tells John to take care of his mother. Life goes on. Past losses do not preclude new opportunities to live and love.

As the ancient *Stabat Mater* hymn says, Mary stood by her son's cross to the very end, even though he had been condemned as a criminal, an outcast. In doing so she is not a pathetic character but a strong person who has taken to heart her son's teaching that we are not to condemn others. She is a strong, full-fledged human being taking her stand with the outsider, the oppressed, the one who has been mockingly treated as a second-class outcast.

It would not be accurate to suggest that the Bible is a "feminist" statement in the modern sense, just as it cannot be said that the Bible takes a stand four-square against the institution of slavery. But the *seeds* of the abolitionist and feminist movements are sown in the Scriptures. While the New Testament writers do not envision the end of the institution of slavery and Saint Paul admonishes a runaway slave to return to his master, Philemon, the New Testament does use the practice of redemption, of buying a slave and then setting him or her free, as a symbol of everything that Jesus accomplishes through his cross. The freeing of slaves becomes a model for the central Christian doctrine of Redemption, and thereby leads inexorably to the ultimate abolition of the entire institution of slavery under the leadership of Christian activists. Saint Paul was not a feminist. In fact, he had an almost embarrassingly patriarchal view of the world. But the insight and inspiration he shares with the Galatians provides the deeper truth which we have come to appreciate more and more today: "There is neither slave nor free, there is neither male nor female; for you are all one in Christ Jesus." (Galatians 3:28)

A recent survey of inactive former church members found that many felt that the church could improve its ministry by "being more accepting of different kinds of people and different lifestyles." One of the most successful churches in San Francisco, Glide Memorial Methodist, celebrates pluralism; and when its pastor, Cecil Williams, received a Social Justice Award he said, "It's dangerous to be just with your own kind . . . the church must say 'I accept you as you are,' not 'I'll accept you when you get like me.' " It has been noted that the "baby-boom" generation tends to be much more accepting of non-traditional life-styles. Must we not face the fact that true mission is not simply the same as promoting tradition? Must we not expand our horizons on what it means to be channels for God's grace?

A woman named Jo Brans has written a book called "Mother, I Have Something to Tell You," in which she discusses the reactions of parents when they discover or are told that their child has an unorthodox life-style or perhaps has not chosen the career that the parents had hoped for. More often than not, she concludes, the appropriate response for the parents is to expand their horizons, to continue to give unconditional love and to try to understand their child. We can create a lot uf unnecessary stress for ourselves by harboring overly-restrictive notions of what constitutes a fulfilling lifestyle.

It seems that a disproportionate number of women are attracted to the kind of metaphysical teachings that have recently found a spokesperson in Shirley MacLaine. She was even asked on the Phil Donahue Show why so few men seem to follow her guidance. Could it be that the world of psychics, palm readers, "past lives" trance channeling, and many other nontraditional movements like Christian Science, tend to be a woman's world because women have been effectively barred from playing major roles in the more traditional Christian churches? Our culture has done a great job of teaching women to express their emotional and intuitive side, but then has failed to take seriously enough the role of feeling and intuition in our theology and our institutions. Walter Wangerin Jr., pastor and author of *The Book of the Dun Cow* and other successful books, has observed that for a majority of Christians, literature is suspect "because it does not seem explicit enough." Many Christians "fear ambiguity," he says, and stories that function more on the level of inference, intuition and emotion, stories about particular people and moments in time, don't seem to meet our need for clear-cut answers. "But then," he adds, "we can meet Christ only in particulars, and it is always in the one we think is the most unlikely."

Which brings us right back to our story about the woman accused of adultery. Even if this were an apocryphal story, we learn as much from it about the message and meaning of the life of Jesus as from any other story or statement in the New Testament. Far from being too simple, too particular or too insignificant because "it's only about a sinful woman, an outcast of low degree," this story teaches in an exquisite way how much God loves and forgives every one of us! This story, along with John's story about the conversation Jesus has with the Samaritan woman at the well (discussing her life and profound issues of theology) shows Jesus to be a person of great feeling, intelligence and intuition — we might even say with no negative stereotype or condescension intended . . . *just like a woman*!

Luke 22:1 — 23:56   Passion Sunday/Palm Sunday

Comfort the Disturbed / Disturb the Comfortable

He stirs up the people teaching . . .

(Luke 23:5)

Years ago many of us celebrated this day as Palm Sunday. It was almost like a mini-Easter — a prelude to the ultimate celebration of the Resurrection. But in recent years we have been reminding ourselves that the more historical name for this day is Passion Sunday. Palm Sunday tended to be a day of waving palm branches, of joy, of singing "Hosannas." Passion Sunday has made the day more like the prelude to Good Friday — a day of somber reflection on the suffering, the *passion*, of our Lord.

The fact is that both names for the day are appropriate. This is above all a day of contrasts, a day of opposites! It is a day of opposite moods — joy . . . and pathos. It is a day of opposite motifs — a "theology of the Cross," . . . and a "theology of glory." It is a day of opposite and mixed messages. On the one hand we celebrate the uplifting and comforting message that we will be with Jesus around the table in his kingdom (Luke 22:30); but on the other hand we are reminded that Jesus does come to rock the boat, that Jesus does "stir people up with his teachings," that Jesus brings both peace and a sword. (Luke 22:36)

During these Sundays of Lent we have been stirred up with some rather intense analysis of what the Christian message and mission is really all about. To some degree we have passed right over some of the finer points of traditional theology — like the subtle differences in various "theories of the Atonement" and "doctrines of Justification" — in favor of a somewhat simplified message founded on the basic meaning of the name "Jesus" itself! It will be totally appropriate for us to argue over whether or not such a simple message of trust in God's grace is an adequate touchstone for Christian identity. We will be totally in keeping with the spirit of Jesus if we are stirred up by discussing and pondering the issues we have been considering and will continue to consider in the Easter season. We should learn from the basic complaint lodged against Jesus in our passion story from Luke, that he was stirring up the people with his teaching. We should learn not to fear and condemn those who stir us up with their message, with their teaching. (You should expect your pastor, your priest, to upset you once in a while! Too many preachers have been reduced to the level of doing little more than humoring people with pious cliches and platitudes, for fear of offending someone.)

You see, there is more than one aspect to being "biblical." One facet of a Bible-based faith is a matter simply of becoming biblically literate. That is, we need to regularly retell the old, old stories. But another aspect of what it means to be biblical is that we should continue to do the kinds of things that the great pioneers of faith did in their day. Just because Abraham left his native land and went west, trusting that God was leading him, does not mean that we must all do exactly the same thing and act as if "go west young man" was a commandment from on high. We do not blindly imitate the actions of Abraham, but we can find our own ways to emulate the faith that gave Abraham the courage to go forward into new and unknown territory. Similarly, we cannot simply quote Jesus as an answer to every problem that confronts us in the modern world. There are many issues on which we have no direct word from the pens of those who have told us stories about Jesus. To be truly biblical is to take a cue from the *kinds of things* that Jesus said and did. Jesus emphasized the spirit of the law as over against the letter of the law, suggesting that to follow the spirit is even more difficult than following the letter. Jesus is constantly pictured as entering into controversy. He is not afraid of stirring people up with his teaching! We should imitate the form and style of what Jesus was about, but some of the actual content of what we say and teach will be new. Jesus got involved in social issues aplenty, but we will look in vain for his comments on what to do when pastors in Pennsylvania become involved in protests over the closing of factories and the resulting unemployment. We can note that Jesus was known to have registered a few dramatic protests of his own — it was on "Palm Sunday" that he went through the cheering crowd, straight to the temple where he proceeded to drive out the established temple business people. (Luke 19:45-46)

One approach that clearly is *not* biblical is to identify one particular religious, political or social ideology as *the Christian* program for creating social justice and the perfect society. This error can manifest itself in any number of ways, including when we start talking about "the Christian candidate" (as if Jesus was running for office) or when we identify the Gospel with unions and socialism as over against capitalism and corporations. Rather than pretending to have all the answers, we should wade into the struggle just as Jesus did and leave the ultimate outcome and judgments to God. The New York pastor, Richard John Neuhaus, has written: "As Christians . . . we have no illusions that we are going to establish a social order of absolute truth and justice here on earth. Our responsibility is to strive for as much truth and as much justice as is possible in a democratic and pluralistic society. And, at the same time, we Christians always should be stretching our society's understanding of what may be possible."

It is extremely difficult to become meaningfully engaged in the struggle for a more just society without self-righteously identifying our partisan understandings and commitments as "the gospel" and any other point of view as "evil." But we must learn from Jesus to leave things somewhat open-ended — as when he said, "Render to Caesar the things that are Caesar's, and to God the things that are God's." (Luke 20:25) The church should never be totally for or totally against a particular society or culture. As Jesus and the prophets were to some degree gadflies in their society, so to a large degree the church must play the role of social critic. We can work for our particular causes with a sense of urgency, but we must face the fact that it will be a rocky road, and devout believers will frequently disagree with each other over goals to some degree and even more so over tactics and methods.

Lord, be my consolation . . . Remind me of thy Passion. (Bernard of Clairvaux)

Jesus preached a message that said "Come unto me all who labor and are heavy laden, and I will give you rest." Jesus came to comfort the disturbed. He understands that we come to church to receive consolation when we are troubled, that we come (as some people say) to "have our batteries recharged for the week." He understands that we come to celebrate the wonder of life and to be inspired by a sermon that reassures and strengthens us. But Jesus was also a teacher. He understands that we also come to remember his Passion, his conflicts. He knows that we need sermons which are part lecture — an opportunity for learning and growing in our understanding of life. Jesus understands that sometimes we are too comfortable and need to be disturbed, to be challenged. His message is also "take my yoke upon you and learn from me." We will discover that his yoke which challenges our complacency, which stimulates us with new ideas and new insights, actually lightens our burdens by helping us to cope with life on a deeper level.

So, this Passion/Palm Sunday is a day of contrasts, and its central figure, Jesus, is a person of contrasts who comes to comfort the disturbed and disturb the comfortable. Of course, we all need to be both comforted and disturbed. And, ironically, we often receive the most effective comfort precisely when we are being disturbed or when we forget about our own need for comfort and express our concern for the suffering of others.

The story has been told for centuries of the Chinese woman who asked a holy man how she could bring her only son who had died back to life. He instructed her to bring him a mustard seed "from a home that has never known sorrow." As she went from home to home, the mansions of the wealthy and the hovels of the poor, she found that there was no such thing as a home that had never known deep sorrow. She became so involved in helping and comforting others in their grief that she forgot all about her quest for the magical mustard seed. To envy others, assuming that they have life easier than we do, is a common misunderstanding of the reality of things. As we know, there was a lot of misunderstanding in that Palm Sunday crowd, and no doubt some folk there were envying Jesus because of all the attention he was getting. Misunderstanding indeed!

The great psychologist, Erich Fromm, was perhaps the first to observe that the phrase "the pursuit of happiness" in the U.S. Constitution is a contradiction in terms. Happiness, he said, never comes when we go out with the deliberate intention of acquiring happiness. Happiness is always the *by-product* of other activities that are meaningful for us. We get busy interacting with other people and the world around us, and, lo and behold, suddenly we realize we are happy. It's the same way with comfort. If we seek it too deliberately as an end in itself it will elude us. But if, with Saint Francis of Assisi, we "seek not so much to be consoled as to console," then we will have it dawn on us that we too are comforted. Lo and behold, as we sing in the Christmas Carol "Silent Night," we will experience "the dawn of redeeming grace."

Luke 22:7-20 (C, L) Maundy Thursday
John 13:1-15 (RC)

Giving Away the Store

He will show you a large upper room furnished.

(Luke 22:12)

If I then, your Lord and Teacher, have washed your feet, you also ought to wash one another's feet.

(John 13:14)

    A friend of mine once had a job briefly at a car rental agency. The job didn't last for long because the owner of the agency complained that my friend was too nice, too diplomatic with the customers. He felt that if my friend were left alone he would probably end up *giving* the cars away — "giving away the store!" The idea behind this expression, "giving away the store," is that if we are too nice to people we won't be in business for long.
    During this Lenten series of messages we have been thinking together about the assertion that it is not our calling as Christians to "win souls for Christ," to get everyone to accept Christianity, to "save the world." It may well appear when we talk in this vein, when we speak of our Christian calling as being simply a matter of channeling God's grace, that we are watering down the Gospel to the point where there is nothing left, that our theology is becoming dangerously simplistic. It may seem that we are giving away the store, giving away too much of the substance of Christian theology and faith. Well, surprise! That's precisely what the Gospel is. The Christian Gospel is a gospel of "giving away the store!" We are called to emulate the self-giving love of Jesus. We are called to absolute humility. There is no room for sanctimoniousness nor boasting! As

Jesus whom we call Lord and Teacher took on the role of a servant and washed the feet of his disciples, so too we are to stop claiming, and start giving. The church is not a storehouse where grace is stored up and sold to those who come bearing the proper coin, namely, a willingness to accept a set of doctrines about Jesus or a rigidly-defined, legalistic lifestyle.

To the degree that we could say that the church and the Word are treasurehouses of God's grace, we are to give away the treasure. But we would actually do better to give up altogether the image of the church as a storehouse of grace in favor of the image of the church, Christians, as *channels* — channels of God's grace as shown to us in the Lord who becomes the servant of all!

Whether we use the image of a channel, or of "giving away the store" is not really the main thing, of course. (We do well to use a great variety of images to express profound truths that are virtually incomprehensible in mere words!) We find another example of free self-giving in this story from Luke 22, where the householder apparently provides the "upper room" free of charge for use by Jesus and his disciples while celebrating the Passover. The message is abundantly clear that the self-emptying, self-giving style of Jesus is contagious. Love really is love only when we give it away! "Maundy Thursday" means "command Thursday," and the command referred to is not only the command to share the bread and wine in remembrance of Jesus, but also to love as he has loved us and to give and serve as he gave and served — and as the householder who furnished the upper room gave freely.

While some might say that defining grace in terms of "giving away the store" is going too far, we need to recognize also that objections have even been raised to the entire theology of grace itself. Such critics maintain that to picture human beings as always helplessly begging for God's grace and mercy is demeaning to our dignity and self-esteem. In his famous classic, *The Golden Bough*, Sir James G. Frazer suggests that religion itself originated from some primitive notion that the gods must be appeased. Frazer's idea is that religion in most of its forms represents a failure of nerve on humankind's part. Originally, primitive peoples tried to manipulate the gods, "the powers that be," to do their bidding through magical rituals that were designed to force the gods to give them what they wanted. When the magic failed to work, people changed their tune and tried instead to find favor with the gods by appeasement, by petition, by pleading for mercy and grace. Frazer and others tend to believe that such a humble posture is unbecoming for a human being. They would not agree with the old aphorism which says that "a person is never so tall as when he is on his knees praying."

Frazer's objection to religion is worth noting because it helps us to clarify what it means to be dependent upon God's grace. Frazer's view of religion emphasizes and focuses upon *power*. God is seen as having the power and human beings must scrape and bow in order to wheedle and coax God into giving them what they need or want. But the view that develops in the New Testament is that our dependence on God is not a matter of power. It is a matter of *relationships*! It is a matter of a mutually loving relationship. "We love because God first loved us." "A new commandment I give to you, that you love one another, even as I have loved you." To speak of God's grace is to speak simply of God's unconditional love. Fundamentally it is not that God demands our submission to divine authority and power. Rather, the example of God's self-giving love moves us to be concerned for justice and love in our relationships with one another. And furthermore, as important as justice and fairness is, ultimately even justice is eclipsed by love in all our relationships with one another and with God. When we suffer with an illness and wonder if life is fair, there comes a point when we realize that the love, faithfulness and support from those around us becomes more important than answering the question of fairness. While some ways of talking about the atonement brought about by the cross of Jesus focus on the satisfaction of God's sense of justice, the overall message of the Gospel of Jesus is that "God is faithful and just *to forgive!*"

God's forgiving love, which always desires to give us a new lease on life, is what "grace" is all about. The most important power and strength that God has and gives to us is the strength to love. Relying upon the mercy and grace of God is not appeasement. It is, rather, learning what love and graciousness mean in all our relationships with one another.

Love consecrates the humblest act . . . Love serves and willing stoops to serve. (S. B. McManus)

In John chapter 13 we read that people will know us as disciples of Jesus if we love one another. Not primarily by right doctrine or concepts, but by love do we show ourselves to be Christians. (Of course this statement itself is the basic "pure doctrine" of the Gospel!) Any doctrinal propositions that obscure the central message of love and grace do not serve us well because they do not move us into a life of loving service. This hymn by S. B. McManus truly captures the essence of the Gospel: "Love consecrates the humblest act and haloes mercy's deeds; it sheds a benediction sweet and hallows human needs. When in the shadow of the Cross Christ knelt and washed the feet of his disciples, he gave us a sign of love complete. Love serves and willing stoops to serve; what Christ in love so true has freely done for one and all, let us now gladly do!"

There are many ways in which we serve in love. We do it by helping people who are in crises. We serve by being sensitive to all the ways in which human beings become victims, and by struggling to perceive and help all victims of poverty, crime, oppression, illness, ignorance. We show love by graciously *accepting* help when *we* need it from those who are in a position to give us aid and comfort. We love when we visit a lonely person and share a little of our time with them. We demonstrate our love when we work for a political cause that we believe will make the world a better place.

To further dispel doubts and objections about whether this giving-away-the-store version of Christianity is a cheapening and weakening of the faith, an inauthentic revision of Christianity, let us turn once more to Luke's account of the Last Supper. In the Revised Standard Version of the New Testament the footnotes to this story tell us that many of the oldest manuscripts do not say anything about the cup as blood and covenant. With a moment's thought it should be obvious why there was and is a problem with linking the cup of wine drunk at Passover with blood. The Jewish Kosher laws were (and are still) mightily concerned to avoid any consumption of the blood of animals. Many Kosher laws are precisely directions on how to properly drain all the blood out of an animal before it is eaten. Therefore, the suggestion that Jesus, a "practicing Jew," would tell his disciples to "drink his blood" is, on its face, ridiculous. In most of the accounts of the Lord's Supper, in fact, Jesus is not pictured as saying "This is my blood." Rather he says "This is the cup of the new covenant *in my blood*." Of course, over time many if not most Christian communities have come to use liturgies that speak of the wine as being the blood of Jesus — "Take and drink. This is my blood." To the extent that we accept the concept of "eating and drinking the body and blood of our Lord" as an appropriate symbol we have to realize that such imagery would have asked Jews to give up one of their most pious notions — the kosher taboo against eating blood. In a sense, to ask Jews to give up this taboo is like asking them to "give away the store."

Here we have an example of how we may sometimes give up a pious and seemingly central belief for the sake of a higher insight and truth. The point in all of these Lenten sermons has been that some of the things we have said and done in our attempt to elevate the name or Jesus have actually served to obscure or misrepresent the true significance of his name. We may need to give up some of our pious notions about evangelism for the sake of a true witness to Jesus.

The task of interpreting the meaning of "believing in Jesus" and his challenge to love as we have been loved is an ongoing commitment. We cannot pretend that there is no need to interpret the Bible. If we did naively take the Bible at face value we would all regularly take part in foot washing ceremonies. But frankly, I don't ever remember washing your feet or having you wash mine! We must interpret. We must be (and *have been*) selective in drawing out what it means to believe in and follow Jesus. To "give away the store" is not to lose faith or to put the Christian church out of business. The church most truly survives when it stops worrying about survival and looks instead for ever new ways to give itself away in humble love and service. "O Master, let me walk with Thee in lowly paths of service free."

To give up our theological delusions of grandeur is not to give up the Gospel. To refine and reinterpret our understanding of what it means to believe in Jesus is not to say that our past ideas and methods of evangelism were all wrong. It is simply to grow and develop in our discernment of what the faith is all about. It is one of the ways in which we *grow in grace*.

John 19:17-30 *Good Friday*

What's Love Got to Do?

> When Jesus saw his mother, and the disciple whom he loved standing near, he said to his mother, "Woman, behold your son!" Then he said to the disciple, "Behold, your mother!" And from that hour the disciple took her to his own home.
>
> (John 19:26-27)

    On this day, the perennial question always arises: "Why do we call this Friday *good*? After all, isn't the crucifixion of Jesus the ultimate triumph of evil? Isn't this event the supreme illustration of the maxim that nice guys finish last? What does this story of a gory execution have to do with love?

    Of course, most of us know the technically correct answers to these questions. We understand that the crucifixion of Jesus is actually the beginning of his exultation. We understand that while the cross on Golgotha symbolizes the ultimate attack of evil upon goodness, it also symbolizes the love of God taking the initiative against evil. When we see Jesus on the Cross, we see what sin does to God, but we also see how God's love and grace confront and overcome sin, despair and evil. We see that, far from being weak and wishy-washy, God's grace is a tower of strength!

    Not long ago a humorous piece of fiction appeared in a newspaper. The writer describes a fellow who wants to create his own little kingdom. It seems this fellow can't decide what title he should give himself. Should he be addressed as "Your Majesty"? Or maybe "Your Excellency"? Someone suggests that he be called "Your Grace," but another advisor objects that such a title would be too "wimpy." It probably is fair to say that many people think of the word or concept of grace as being namby-pamby, soft, unmanly. (Some might even crassly accuse Jesus of being "just a wimp with a martyr complex"!)

But grace is not a wimp word and Jesus is anything but a wimp! It takes great strength to love, to forgive, to understand rather than to blame and condemn. To be gracious is to balance strength with mercy, justice with love. The old illustration of the oak and the willow is a good one. The mighty oak is so strong that it never bends in a strong wind, but it may break. The willow tree, on the other hand, may bend in a wind but it will not break. By being firm yet flexible, the willow may be better off in the long run. So it is with grace. God's grace is firm yet flexible. It has a strength that goes beyond mere brute force. The grace that we see in Jesus is like the gentle strength of a dolphin. The wrath of God is not so much a negative force against sin and evil as it is a strong, driving force towards goodness and love. We all recognize this invocation from its frequent use in our worship services: "The grace of our Lord Jesus Christ be with you all." I am happy to report that another similar invocation is also becoming popular: "In the strong name of Jesus!"

Now, of course, all this talk about grace and love *would* be wimpy and namby-pamby *without the Cross*! Without the Cross, free grace would become cheap grace. By always connecting the grace and love of God with the story of the crucifixion of Jesus it becomes crystal clear that the Christian faith is anything but naive about the reality of evil, sin and death. What's love got to do with Good Friday? It has to do with God's self-giving struggle against evil, sin and death, on our behalf.

In some of the other religions and philosophies of the world there is a tendency not to take evil seriously. Some say, for example, that evil is only a delusion of the carnal mind — that if we were only spiritually-minded enough we would realize that evil isn't real. The New Testament takes the reality of this material world much more seriously than that and calls us to become involved in the struggle to make this world a better place. Our prayer is "Thy will be done *on earth* as it is in heaven." Evil is real, and real effort must be put forth in order to defeat it.

As we observed at the beginning of this lenten series, the struggle to do the will of God is difficult and requires strength in more ways than one. In 1910 G.K. Chesterton wrote, "The Christian ideal has not been tried and found wanting; it has been found difficult and left untried." Yet challenging as it is to *do* the will of God, it can be an even bigger problem to discover what the will of God is in the first place. Religious and moral people have displayed a tendency to strain out gnats and swallow camels! We can easily fall into the trap of focusing our attention on relatively insignificant and debatable points while virtually ignoring the truly important issues. A magazine article once displayed two pictures placed side by side. One picture showed a beautiful woman scantily clad. The other picture was of a corpse from a Nazi concentration camp. The caption under the two pictures read: "Which of these photos is obscene?" The stories of the Holocaust and of the crucifixion of Jesus both remind us of what can happen when we fail to keep our ethical priorities straight, when we strain out gnats and swallow camels.

Lift high the cross . . . So shall our song of triumph ever be: Praise to the Crucified for victory! (Kitchin and Newbolt)

Above all, to celebrate Good Friday is to redefine the concept of victory!

A few years ago the Rev. Robert Schuller produced a TV program about amputee skiers entitled "The Bravest Athletes in the World." (The fact that his own daughter had recently lost a leg in an accident no doubt helped to spark his interest.) At the conclusion of the program the point was made that "anyone who really tries is a winner." Now no one can criticize the basic idea behind that statement. But why does the notion of "winning" have to be the gauge against which everything is measured? Why not simply say that anyone who really tries can feel good about himself or herself, can celebrate the joy of participating? Why not say that anyone who really tries is truly *alive to life*! There is a lot of truth in the old saying that it's not whether you win or lose but how you play the game that counts. And the saying is particularly true when we apply it to "the game of life."

Lily Tomlin likes to joke that even if you win the rat race, you're still a rat. An ethic that puts too much emphasis on winning easily leads to cynicism about the value of honesty, easily turns into the attitude of "success at any cost." Such basic human values as loyalty, caring and justice tend to lose out when we adopt the mentality of the rat race.

Kathleen Speath and Ira Friedlander, in their book about the famous Russian philosopher of religion, George Gurdjieff, observe that his life "whether at the bottom line a success or failure in the attainment of his aims was certainly of noble proportions." Many of the great people who have positively influenced the course of human history were not what we would call winners. Mozart, for example, has made an incalculable contribution to our culture, but he was unceremoniously dumped into a pauper's grave when he died at the age of 35.

The victory of Good Friday is nothing other than the triumph of life over death. It has little or nothing to do with winning. To be able to affirm life in spite of all the reasons not to do so — *that* is true victory! From the Cross, Jesus looks at his beloved friend and disciple, John, and tells him to adopt his mother, Mary, as his own mother. In the midst of death, Jesus shows his concern for the continuation of life by turning his attention to his mother. What better way to affirm life than by affirming motherhood — (an obvious symbol of life)? Far from wishing that he had never been born, Jesus recognizes that it is for this very moment that he has been born — to affirm life in the face of death.

It continues to boggle the mind of many people that Christians sing "Lift high the cross . . . So shall our song of triumph ever be! Praise to the Crucified for victory!" What does the Cross of Jesus have to do with love and victory?

The Cross is the sign and seal of God's involvement in our struggle with the multifaceted reality of this world, including the dark side of life. The story of the Cross makes it possible for us to conquer despair, to enter into the struggles of life with faith and courage and to become, like Jesus, channels of the love and grace of God.

John 20:1-18

Will the Real Jesus Christ Arise?

"We do not know where they have laid him" . . . Jesus said to her, "Do not hold me, for I am about to ascend to my Father."

(John 20:2b, 17a)

You may remember the television program "To Tell The Truth." Three people would come out, all claiming to be the same person. After the panel had interviewed all three and everyone had decided who the imposters were, the host would intone dramatically: "Will the *real* John Doe, please stand up!" Then everyone waited with baited breath as each contestant stirred as if to rise until, finally, the real person did stand up.

In the *New York Times Magazine*, December 23, 1973, Fr. Andrew Greeley, in an article entitled "What Kind of Man?" made it clear that not everyone agrees when it comes to the question of who is the real Jesus Christ. Some think of him as a pietistic fundamentalist, or superpatriot, or the ultimate "positive thinker." Others have painted him as a revolutionary or anti-establishment hippie — possibly a Zealot or a counterculture Essene who had sought purity in a desert monastery like the one at which the Dead Sea Scrolls were discovered. Still others have tried to make him into an ecclesiastical bureaucrat, a member of the temple priesthood.

Greeley himself concludes that Jesus was most probably associated with a left-wing group of liberal *Pharisees* described in the Talmud as the "Pharisees of Love." Unlike their legalistic counterparts whom Jesus often criticized severely, these Pharisees were religious revolutionaries and poetic visionaries who challenged people to new visions and new understandings of their traditions. Most notably, they believed in the Resurrection of the dead, a belief that had not been common among Jews for most of their history. Greeley is not alone in this view that Christianity might best be understood as an outgrowth of the Pharisaic movement with its radical new belief in Resurrection.

Another recent suggestion is that the real Jesus Christ was not a solemn, sad-eyed ascetic but a fun-loving and joyous person. A famous painting of "the laughing Jesus" has become quite popular, and it may well be a good antidote to the many overly-serious portraits which artists have imagined. Jesus has also been described as a "religious genius," and, as you might guess, this image of Jesus was put forward by an academically-oriented person. We have also seen of late a popular tendency to identify Jesus with Buddha or other great religious figures, as if Jesus and Buddha and Confucius, for example, are all just different manifestations of the same spiritual being. In 1986 the famous church historian at Yale University, Jaroslav Pelikan, published a book titled *Jesus Through The Centuries*, subtitled "His Place in the History of Culture." The book jacket says that it is about "the changing image of Jesus in Western civilization within cultural, political, social and economic realms." And, certainly no discussion of the search for "the real Jesus Christ" would be complete without also mentioning Albert Schweitzer's classic book, *The Quest for the Historical Jesus*.

Beginning on this Easter Day we embark upon a series of sermons that ask the fundamental question: "Will the Real Jesus Christ Arise?" What about all these theories concerning the "Real Jesus"? Are we all just raising up our own notions of who Jesus really is or are we honestly listening to history and the Scriptures as they speak to us of this person named Jesus and his association with the title of Christ?

Not long before his untimely death, the gifted theologian and bishop, Kent Knutson, introduced one of his books with these words: "This is a book about Jesus Christ. It is rather presumptuous to write such a book. Suitable books are already available. The one by John in the New Testament, for example . . . [But] John himself says [that] no book can do Christ justice." Having said this, Knutson then launches into a discussion of some of the basic doctrines about Jesus Christ, emphasizing above all that "the Jesus of history must remain united with the Christ of faith." Clearly it is an important but difficult task to understand what it means to say that

Jesus is the Christ, the Messiah, but it is an ongoing responsibility for those of us who claim the name of Christian!

In telling the story of the resurrection of Jesus, John's Gospel consistently emphasizes the point that Jesus is *gone*! In our text for today Mary Magdalene discovers at the tomb that Jesus is gone and she tells Peter, "We do not know where they have laid him." This uncertainty about where Jesus has gone must continue to be for us yet today a powerful reminder of the fact that the meaning of the Resurrection of Jesus remains in many respects a great *mystery*! In many ways, the Christian church is built entirely upon our interpretations of the *absence* of Jesus. Especially in John the point is made that Jesus has to go away so that we will be forced to do a lot of wondering about his identity, so that we will begin to understand whole new dimensions of his continuing presence with us. When, a little later, Jesus tells Mary not to hold or touch him because he is about to go away, we are reminded of the other places in John's Gospel where Jesus says that it is *good* for him to go away because if he doesn't go away he cannot send the Spirit or "prepare a place for us." The departure of Jesus — our inability to hold on to him — is not unfortunate. It is the prerequisite for his continuing presence with us in a great variety of forms.

Complementing the thought that we must not try to hold onto Jesus in his physical form, is this earlier observation in verses 8-9 "The other disciple, who reached the tomb first [and this, by the way is John himself] also went in, and he saw and believed; for as yet they did not know the Scripture, that he must rise from the dead." Now, what did this disciple believe if he did not yet fully understand "resurrection"? The answer is clear that the meaning of the resurrection of Jesus unfolded slowly, like a flower. Although through time-lapse photography we can watch a flower suddenly spring into its full glory, the actual development takes longer. In some ways at least, the same has been true with respect to the New Testament faith in the Resurrection. Today, with the advantage of hindsight, we may think of the Resurrection as an event whose meaning sprang suddenly to light, whereas, in fact, even the apostles and writers of the Gospels did not immediately understand "that he must rise from the dead." Bishop Knutson was right in saying that we must not think of ourselves as qualitatively more knowledgeable than the New Testament evangelists. It is still true for us, as it was for them, that much of what we believe only dawns upon us slowly, by degrees.

Our understanding — our comprehension — is incomplete. We believe, even though the full ramifications of our faith remain yet to be realized.

In the Gospel of John and elsewhere in the New Testament the resurrection of Jesus is intimately connected with the theme of his absence and the necessity of his reappearance or "second coming" (the *parousia.*) The Greek word literally means the "being again" of Jesus. Whether we use the terms "second coming," "second presence," "reappearance," or even "reincarnation" of Jesus, the fundamental truth remains the same, namely, that although gone, Jesus is able to *be again* (parousia) *with us* (emmanuel)! Just as there is an element of truth in many of the characterizations of "the real Jesus Christ" that Fr. Greeley and others have highlighted for us, so too there are many aspects to the resurrection of Jesus. The Resurrection sets the stage for many kinds of resurrection appearances and second comings of Jesus, the Christ.

Every Advent and Christmas we celebrate the coming of Christ and we could say that we have already enjoyed almost 2000 of these reappearances! In the Gospel of Mark the coming of Jesus is associated not with his birth but with the beginning of his ministry after his baptism in the river Jordan — already a kind of "second" coming. The story of the Transfiguration could be described as "a pre-Easter resurrection appearance." The various accounts of resurrection appearances placed after the death of Jesus make it clear that his reappearance takes a variety of forms. One of those forms is the Holy Spirit who, according to John's Gospel, will take the place of Jesus as our Counselor when Jesus is no longer physically present with us. The Sacraments are another form in which Jesus continues to come again to us . . . and, Jesus truly comes to us again and again whenever his Gospel is preached and whenever we behave as "little Christs" toward our neighbors — helping each other and struggling to understand each other as we would like to be understood. Then, of course, there are all the various notions of the second coming of Christ at the end of time. Clearly, having gone away, Jesus continually comes and reappears in our lives.

There is grace enough for thousands of new worlds as great as this; there is room for fresh creations in that upper home of bliss.
(Fredrick W. Faber)

There is, however, one way of talking about the resurrection or reappearance of Jesus which needs to be seriously questioned. Given the recent surge of interest in past lives, trance channeling and reincarnation, we need to take note of the reasons why the Christian faith has consistently resisted describing the resurrection, reappearance or second coming of Christ in terms of reincarnation. Christianity has a basically positive attitude toward the material world and toward our physical bodies and puts great stress on the *Incarnation* of God in the form of Jesus, so why the tendency to shy away from the idea of *re*incarnation?

First of all, we need to understand that we do not truly foster religious unity by homogenizing the divergent teachings of the world's religions into one composite view and pretending that real differences don't exist. We create more honest unity and understanding by entering into humble dialogue and debate about important and meaningful distinctions than we do by glossing over differences.

The Jewish concept of Sheol, the Greek idea of the immortality of the soul, the Christian belief in the resurrection, and the Hindu/Buddhist doctrine of reincarnation are significantly different! *Sheol* is the idea that all the dead go to one neutral place and that's it. They are, simply, dead. The typical concept of *immortality* is that a part of us never dies and lives on after death. *Reincarnation* is the belief that a single soul takes many forms and enters into many bodies, many forms, throughout its existence.

Resurrection, in contrast to all of these ideas, suggests that when we die we are *really dead*, but, miraculously, God is able to create new life out of death. One of the main things that distinguishes the Christian belief in the resurrection from both the Greek and Hindu philosophies is that it takes the physical fact of death seriously. It refuses to whitewash death, refuses to belittle the grief that we experience when death comes. The Christian concept of resurrection makes us wary of trite, shallow reassurances in the face of death. Pious platitudes can actually do more harm than good when they are substituted for an honest encounter with grief. It may be partly true to say to a grieving friend, "You'll get over it in time" or "Death is just a transition — it's not the end of the world." But this kind of well-intentioned comfort really is not helpful. We are in effect telling the person that we do not take their pain, their loss, their grief, seriously! We do better to tell them, by words or actions, what they really need and want to hear — that we recognize our inability to even imagine how much they are hurting. In one of his more profound *Peanuts* comic strips, Charles Schulz shows Lucy offering to do anything to cheer up Charlie Brown. Finally in exasperation Charlie shouts "I don't *want* to feel better!" When we are in pain the meanest thing a person can do is to belittle our suffering.

The second thing we need to be clear about is that the Hindu/Buddhist doctrine of reincarnation and the Christian notion of resurrection came into being in radically different contexts and for quite different reasons. The world-view behind reincarnation is that life is an endless cycle of death and reincarnation, and that the ultimate goal is to escape from the world of physical bodies into Nirvana — to be absorbed into God and to cease to exist as a separate entity. Reincarnation talks a lot about the physical body, but doesn't really take it seriously!

Reincarnation is also tied together with the doctrine of Karma, which is mainly designed to prove that life is fair (in the long run we all get what we deserve and everything happens for a reason.) In stark contrast, the Christian understanding of resurrection and of the grace of God is intended to deal precisely with the fact that *life is not fair*! While we must work as hard as possible to "establish justice in the earth," never using the apparent unfairness of life as an excuse for not struggling to make life as fair as we can make it, the Christian message is that in the last analysis some things are simply more important than fairness. God's love and grace go far beyond simply seeing that we get what we deserve. Love transcends logic. Ultimately the fairness of life becomes an academic question. What we really care about is that we not be left alone when the going gets rough. In the movie based on the life of Terry Fox, the young man who ran two-thirds of the way across Canada on an artificial leg, the most poignant scene comes when a resurgence of the cancer stops the marathon and puts Terry back in the hospital. His father finally breaks down and says through his tears "It isn't fair!" Terry responds: "It's fair. There are a lot of people who have this happen to them who don't deserve it. It's not a matter of fair or unfair. It's just the way things are." What really matters to Terry at this point is that he is surrounded by the love and concern of his family and friends, that he is not left alone.

Reincarnation is primarily about fairness. Resurrection is primarily about defeating the power of death. Resurrection is about affirming life in the face of all the reasons not to — including the fact that life is often unfair and capricious. The stories of the resurrection of Jesus show us that life, and love, and the grace and faithfulness of God eclipse all other values. The only thing which would be truly unfair would be not to be loved!

Above all perhaps, the problem with the traditional concept of reincarnation is that it believes both too much and too little! By suggesting that life is just a recycling of what we already know, that past lives and future lives are not that different from this life, reincarnationists claim to know more about life in other dimensions than it is really possible for us to know. They believe "too much." We can also turn this observation around and say that reincarnational logic believes "too little." Most who espouse reincarnation do speak about other "plains" or dimensions of reality, but it seems that they do so too much in terms of our present experience of life. Profoundly challenging paradoxes like Saint Paul's vision of a "spiritual body" rarely come to the fore among reincarnationists. Like some Christians who have the mundane notion that heaven is little more than streets of gold and family reunions, they believe *too little*, because they are not open enough to the possibility of *the new*. Even when reincarnation is translated from its Hindu self-*negating* context into the language of the human potential movement and presented as the path by which we reach our fullest self-*realization*, there is not enough openness to the likelihood that the other dimensions of life are far beyond anything we can possibly understand now — even if we did have some kind of spirit guide!

The resurrection of Jesus speaks to us of the exciting new possibilities of life coming from the Creator. While it is not typically associated with Easter, Frederick Faber's hymn "There's a Wideness in God's Mercy" wonderfully catches the spirit of this resurrection newness: "There is grace enough for thousands of new worlds as great as this; there is room for fresh creations In that upper home of bliss." In his famous theological system, Paul Tillich described Jesus as "the New Being." The *real Jesus* arises when we stop trying to make Jesus into a recycled version of our pet notions about him and allow God to make Jesus, us, and all things, *new*!

John 20:19-31   Easter 2

Colorizing Jesus

The doors were shut, but Jesus came and stood among them, and said . . . "Blessed are those who have not seen and yet believe."

(John 20:26b, 29b)

Most of us are familiar with the controversy that has been going on over the issue of "colorizing" old black-and-white movies. Do Humphrey Bogart and the *Maltese Falcon* or Jimmy Stewart and his *Wonderful Life* look better in the original black-and-white photography or with color added by one of the latest wrinkles in computer technology?

There is a strong parallel between the discussion of colorizing old movies and the discussion that has gone on for centuries in the Christian church, over the issue of the divinity of Jesus — a discussion that has resulted in the classic doctrine of the "two Natures" of Christ. The creeds of the church traditionally teach that, in addition to his human nature, Jesus also has the added dimensions of a divine nature. Jesus has been, if you will, "colorized." The historical "Jesus" is the black-and-white original. The biblical "Christ" is the colorized version.

Now while all analogies admittedly break down at some point, this one can be helpful for us. Color is a marvelous part of life. It is a perfect symbol for those rich and oftentimes indefinable dimensions of reality that literally make life what it is. Through the centuries the church has said in effect that there are many ineffable dimensions or colorations to the life of Jesus which go beyond the basic black-and-white facts of the historical person of Jesus.

To put it another way, Jesus is much more than a human being. The Real Jesus is as much a *Symbol* as he is a person! He is the ultimate symbol for the grace of God, and as John describes him, the ultimate personification of Truth with a capital T.

It is important to acknowledge that this kind of talk is more controversial than it may sound. At the conclusion of this story about the famous "doubting Thomas," we read these words (which should be equally famous although, unfortunately, they probably are not): "Now Jesus did many other signs in the presence of his disciples, which are not written in this book; but these are written that you may believe that Jesus is the Christ, the Son of God, and that believing you may have life in his name." (vv. 30-31) These words have immense importance, because they remind us that the Gospels of Matthew, Mark, Luke and John are not, properly speaking, biographies of Jesus. The writers have *selected* what they believe will accomplish their purpose, which is to give a specific *interpretation* of who Jesus is and what his life means for us all.

We must, therefore, learn to live with the distinction between Jesus as an historical person, and Jesus as a *symbolic, literary figure*. Each Gospel presents us with its own unique portrait (in color!) of Jesus. This explains why there are many striking differences — and, yes, we even have to say, discrepancies — between these various accounts of the life and ministry of Jesus. Strictly speaking, the Gospels are theological interpretations of Jesus, not newspaper-like reports of the mere facts. We have tended to underestimate the role of the New Testament writers and editors in creating Jesus as we know him.

Many of us who stand in pulpits have learned that it is somewhat misleading to use the expression "Jesus says" as if we were always dealing with a simple and direct quote. We know that we really should rather say something like "the Gospel of Luke pictures Jesus as saying . . ." or that we should speak in terms of "Mark's Jesus" or "Matthew's Jesus." But more often than not it seems that we are afraid to express ourselves in a way that inevitably brings up this whole issue of Jesus as a literary figure created by the Gospel editors, as over against Jesus as simply an historical person. We recognize the truth in the observation made by the Stanford University professor of religion, Frederic Spiegelberg. He wrote that the emphasis put upon the historicity of Jesus may be a major key to the success of Christianity. We do not in any way want to give the impression that the stories about Jesus are little more than fairy tales.

But when the editors of John's Gospel tell us that they have chosen to write about certain things in order to make us believe that Jesus is the Christ, we must face the fact that they are literally creating their own version of Jesus. They are doing the same thing that we have been doing when we have asked what it *means* to believe in Jesus — they are interpreting what his life means for us. The New Testament presents us with a particular reinterpretation of the Messiah-concept as passed on to us by this remarkable new movement within Judaism, the early Christian community.

What follows is a factual story. There once was a seminary student who was having a hard time accepting this idea that the writers of the New Testament Gospels took poetic license with their accounts of the life of Jesus. He was particularly bothered by the extreme view of some scholars that Jesus *might* not have been an actual historical person at all! One day as a fellow student was playing around with his tape recorder, the two suddenly fell into a spontaneous mock interview with the troubled student pretending to be "professor Rudolf Boltloose" (a parody of the famous German biblical scholar, Rudolf Bultmann). Piously, professor "Boltloose" intoned — "I have come up with a new theory! There was no cross at calvary. There were only nails. There was no body. There were only clothes. You see, they hung the clothes on the nails . . . *And this is important for us today!*" Although totally spontaneous, this little episode of play-acting was a superb statement of the danger we face when we deal with the fact that the Gospels are not biographies of Jesus.

The fact that there are dangers, however, cannot prevent us from coming to terms with the tension between Jesus as an historical person and Jesus as a literary figure created by the inspired New Testament writers, the tension between the "historical Jesus" and the "biblical Christ." While we go too far off the deep end if we conclude that the stories about Jesus are like fairy tales, nothing more than "cleverly devised myths," we also go off the deep end if we assume that Jesus was simply a man whose straightforward biography is preserved in the New Testament.

To highlight the issue for you, let me risk shaking you up a bit by picturing one of the more radical views of how Christianity originated. The suggestion is made that perhaps Jesus was not one individual man, but that he is a composite character created by the Gospel writers to summarize their teachings. There were many crosses and many crucifixions in Palestine during the Roman occupation. Travelers walking down the road might encounter hundreds of crosses lining the way with various political and other "criminals" being put to death by the occupying forces. How could one maintain faith and hope and love in the midst of such a holocaust? By telling the story of an innocent victim of crucifixion who is vindicated by God through the kind of resurrection espoused among the Pharisees, that's how! Is not the miracle of the Christian faith precisely and simply that it affirms the grace and love of God in spite of all the reasons not to do so, that it affirms life in stark defiance of the grim reality of death?

While there is no good reason to doubt that Jesus was an actual historical person, it is most instructive to contemplate the possibility that Christian faith could be *true* regardless of the facts of the case. Ultimately, don't we have to recognize that truth goes far beyond mere facts. When John pictures Jesus as saying to Thomas, "Blessed are those who have not seen and yet believe," is he not clearly making the point that historical facts in and of themselves cannot really *prove* anything?

In 1984 David Jenkins, the newly consecrated bishop of Durham, England, created what was and still is a healthy controversy, by publicly questioning whether the resurrection of Jesus is primarily a physical reality or the eruption into our world "of a new reality that changes our approach to all reality." Some critics said that such discussions belong only in the classroom where academic theologians can debate, and that it is poor judgment and poor public relations for church leaders to bring such issues into public discussion. Well, a few years earlier another Anglican bishop, John A.T. Robinson, wrote a book called *Honest to God*, in which he clearly made a conscious decision to open up such dialogue among all Christians, on such subjects as the status of the Bible and the nature of belief. Such matters are, (to borrow a phrase) "too important to leave to the experts." And as for controversy itself, must we not agree that healthy controversy is much better than stagnant blandness?

Perhaps the clearest expression of this tension between the historical Jesus and the biblical Christ is to be seen in the way John's Gospel vacillates between presenting the risen Jesus as a physical being who urges Thomas to place his finger into the nail prints in his wrists, and presenting the risen Jesus as a Spirit who is able to pass through solid, locked doors. ("The doors were shut, but Jesus came and stood among them . . .") Again, in Luke's Gospel, the risen Jesus eats a fish to demonstrate that he has flesh and blood, but he also vanishes as into thin air following his encounter with the two disciples on the road to Emmaus. Clearly, the physical, historical

Jesus is not the primary reality! The risen Jesus is not understood to be simply a resuscitated corpse. The black-and-white, historical Jesus has been colorized. The real Jesus Christ is the reinterpreted, risen Christ who, paradoxically, both affirms and transcends the physical world.

"Grace which like the Lord, the Giver, never fails from age to age."
(John Newton)

Why is it important for us not to think of Jesus too exclusively in physical or historical terms? One reason, again, is that the Bible continually reminds us that the object of our faith goes beyond what can be seen, "Blessed are those who have not seen and yet believe," because they realize that faith has a mysterious side which both affirms and yet transcends the physical dimension. But perhaps the greatest problem with over-emphasizing the historical uniqueness of Jesus is that it tends to make Jesus into a kind of lucky charm. Such an emphasis can lead to the wrong type of Christ-centeredness, in which all theological meaning goes by the wayside and nothing is left but an icon, an idol. Soon we resort to saying, Forget what it *means* to believe in Jesus — just as long as you *have* him."

Fundamentally we do not have Jesus as a lucky charm, but rather as a *symbol* of the unconditional grace and love of God. The reason it *is* important to stress the historicity of Jesus is that the historical Jesus provides the framework for a unique and radical theology of grace. The "scandal of particularity" in Christianity proclaims that the grace of God has been revealed in a special way through Jesus, the Christ, in contrast to Buddha, for example. It is historically dishonest to pretend that Buddha and Jesus are the same, because the two figures come out of profoundly different contexts. The "scandal" is not that Jesus claims to be better than Buddha, but simply that the *particular* New Testament understanding of Jesus as the Christ gives a unique flavor (or color!) to the meaning of God's grace. Without this particular flavor/color, the "grace of God" too easily becomes just some vague substance floating, so to speak, in the air. As we have seen, true unity between Christians and Buddhists (and others) can best come about when we enter into dialogue with one another, sharing our unique insights into the meaning of the grace of God and allowing our distinctively different flavors to complement one another.

We need to hold onto our sense of the historical uniqueness of Jesus, then, because Jesus is more than some vague, nebulous symbol for grace, and because it is not truly helpful in the long run to blur together such different concepts as reincarnation and resurrection. But we must also live with the awareness that as the Christ, Jesus is a kind of "everyman" or "everyperson" who symbolizes the unity of all people. On this level it is appropriate for each ethnic group to picture Jesus as looking like them — an Asian Jesus for Asians, an Indian Jesus for Indians, and the like.

Furthermore, to say that Jesus is a unique symbol for the grace of God does not take away from the fact that Buddhism also emphasizes grace. (Zen, "Pure Land" and Amida Buddhism in particular understand salvation as a gift that is given, not earned.) To say that Jesus is a unique channel of God's grace is simply to say that Jesus is as close as one can come to the embodiment of God's grace! Jesus is the strongest possible symbol for that "grace which like the Lord, the Giver, Never fails from age to age."

If all of this just sounds like confusing double-talk to you, if you would rather relate to a Jesus who is simple and one-dimensional, who comes in only one color (or in black-and-white), maybe this true story will help you better to cope with these ambiguous and perhaps threatening distinctions between the historical Jesus and the literary/biblical Christ, between faith that tries to rest mainly upon mere facts and faith that sees truth beyond or in spite of the facts. A famous actress tells the story of a friend of hers whose handsome movie star husband was slowly wasting away from a terrible disease. One day her friend came to visit and began lamenting the fact that she was at her wit's end. "Can't you suggest to me some quote from the Bible or somewhere that will help me get through this ordeal?" she pleaded. Caught off guard, the actress couldn't think of a quote but said she would think about it and try to come up with something. The next day, her friend called and excitedly told her, "I've got my quote!" "What is it?" "It's from Shakespeare . . . *Macbeth*: 'Tomorrow, and tomorrow, and tomorrow, Creeps in this petty pace from day to day, To the last syllable of recorded time.' " "How can you find any solace in that dark sentiment?" the actress exclaimed. "I find it wonderfully helpful precisely because it does not try to comfort me," her friend replied. "It simply reminds me that long before me and long after me people have dealt with such trials and have survived."

In spite of his obvious awareness of the dark side of life, in spite of his struggle with the ambiguity of life, Shakespeare basically continued to celebrate life. He has enriched all of our lives — he has colored our world with the beauty and insight of his words. The real, colorized Jesus Christ likewise shines through the ambiguity and confusion of our world and rises to meet us with the assurance of tomorrows yet undreamed of.

Peace be with you who have not seen, and yet believe.

John 21:1-14 *Easter 3*

Throw Your Heart at the Sky

> *Just as day was breaking, Jesus stood on the beach; yet the disciples did not know that it was Jesus . . . Now none of the disciples dared ask him, "Who are you?" They knew it was the Lord.*
>
> (John 21:4, 12b)

Now wait a minute! Either they knew it was Jesus or they didn't. Why would it even occur to them to ask who he was if they already *knew* who it was? The answer is that the editors of the gospel of John (and many scholars think that John went through at least three major revisions) are using this story to show once again that the full impact and meaning of the resurrection of Jesus dawned upon his followers progressively, in stages, over time. By saying that this was the third time Jesus was revealed to the disciples after he was raised from the dead (v. 14), by combining it with an element of confusion over whether they recognized Jesus or not (vv. 4 and 12), and by setting the whole episode in the context of the dawning of a new day, the editors are driving home the point that the ressurection faith of the early Christian movement developed gradually.

There may be an element of suddenness to the resurrection of Jesus. After all, we *do* ultimately base our faith more on Jesus than on a group of editors! But the strong association of Easter with the symbolism of the dawn reminds us that the gradual unfolding of resurrection faith is an equally valid component of the equation. The arising of the real Jesus Christ has indeed already happened. But it also continues to happen in a variety of ways. The meaning of the resurrection of Jesus is by no means diminished when we make honest efforts to interpret the New Testament correctly and when we resist the temptation to read into it only what we wish to see there. To ask "Will the real Jesus Christ arise?" is a way of reminding ourselves continually to question our pet theories about the Christian faith, so that we will not lose touch with the true Gospel of the grace of God.

We have used the image of "colorizing Jesus" to make it clear that the real Jesus is a complex, multi-dimensional Jesus. It should no longer bother us to read an article like the one that appeared recently in a major church journal reporting on a "Jesus Seminar" at which New Testament scholars voted on the authenticity of sayings attributed to Jesus. We understand that the purpose of such a seminar is not to question the authority of the Bible, but to keep us aware of the distinction between the historical person of Jesus and the images or interpretations of Jesus created by the authors and editors of the New Testament. The question of the authenticity of the sayings of Jesus is basically just a question of the degree of poetic license employed by the early Christian writers. Sometimes they borrowed sayings from much earlier sources and put them on the lips of Jesus. Many literary conventions were used in the effort to present an authentic portrait of the Gospel of Jesus Christ.

We can also appreciate the goals for the above-mentioned seminar stated by its organizer, New Testament scholar Robert Funk. They were, he said, "to combat the 'pious platitudes' of television evangelists and the doomsday writings of modern apocalypticists . . . and to report the assured results of historical-critical scholarship to a broader public." (By the way, one of the better recent books that explains contemporary biblical scholarship for the general public is Richard E. Friedman's *Who Wrote the Bible?*, Summit Books.)

Nor should it bother us to recognize that there is a lot of symbolism in the Gospel of John and in our story for today. We know that the Gospel of John starts out by borrowing the rather abstract Greek concept of the *Logos* to explain the meaning of Jesus: Jesus is the ultimate expression of the divine *principle* of creation. Jesus is the ultimate Symbol of symbols! Our story in chapter 21 clearly symbolizes the missionary commission to be "fishers of men." While there are many possible explanations for the number of fish caught being 153, a most likely one refers to a common notion in those days that there were a total of 153 varieties of fish. The symbolism, therefore, is that, in the words of G.H.C. MacGregor, "the Gospel net is to embrace every conceivable variety of men" — and it will not tear in the process! The modern term is "inclusive ministry."

Let every heart prepare him room . . . He rules the world with Truth and Grace (Isaac Watts)

Yet, although John is a complex and symbolic Gospel, it is also for many people their favorite Gospel because of its warm, personal and "spiritual" tone. Jesus is indeed complex and multi-dimensional, but there is also a sense in which Jesus is a model of wonderful simplicity. Jesus has always been a symbol of *personal* faith. Paradoxically, Jesus has always symbolized resistance to the kind of religion that is a mere collection of abstract symbols. The Christmas message of "God made flesh" is a symbol of moving beyond *mere* symbolism to a personal relationship with the Creator. At Christmas we sing "Joy to the world . . . let every heart prepare him room . . . He rules the world with Truth and Grace." Jesus is the symbol of Living Truth that warms our hearts with the personal assurance of God's all-encompassing Grace and Love.

Many great thinkers, such as Spinoza, have thought of God as nothing more than an abstract, mathematical symbol of that system which is the universe. God becomes just another word for The Universe. But when John's Gospel has Jesus say "I am the Way, the Truth, and the Life," the personal nature of truth is being driven home. Truth is a *person*, not a set of ideas! To know God through Jesus Christ is to know God in a personal way.

Professor William Streng, who taught for many years at Wartburg Theological Seminary in Dubuque, Iowa, used to satirize folks who were doggedly learning the concepts taught by the Bethel Bible Series. He would describe them as unsympathetically pushing aside a person in need — "Get out of my way! I've got to get to the church to learn my Bible concepts!" Dr. Streng understood John's message that the Truth is personal, that Truth is a way of behaving, an attitude of mind and not just a set of ideas. Jesus does not answer Pilate's question, "What is truth?" because Pilate has already demonstrated his inability to perceive Truth embodied in the person standing before him. Jesus is a person of integrity, honesty, perception, love and innocence — and Pilate does not see it! No words or concepts will break through his spiritual blindness. We all know the saying "Actions speak louder than words." That is a large part of what John means when he says that Jesus is the living embodiment of Truth.

Another example of impersonal thinking getting in the way of personal truth would be the issue of ordaining gay people. The subject is usually discussed as if such ordinations would be something radically new, whereas, in fact, there have been and are countless gay clergy, many of them significant leaders in the church. Because gay religious professionals are understandably hesitant to let their sexual orientation be known due to the potential for discrimination, most church people do not realize that they actually know many gay people personally — and like them! They continue to think of homosexuals and lesbians in terms of some abstract *idea* of "perversion." The personal truth, I believe, is that once you get to know gay people personally, your prejudices about sexual orientation quickly begin to melt away. An encounter with a real person brings out the truth that dissolves inaccurate, unfair and stereotypical ideas.

One of the problems with conceiving of truth merely in terms of ideas and concepts is that truth is too dynamic and paradoxical to be nailed down. Truth is alive and moving. Someone has said, "Our highest truths are but half truths. Think not to settle down forever in any truth. Make use of it as a tent in which to pass a summer's night. But build no house of it, or it will be your tomb. When you first have an inkling of its insufficiency and begin to decry a dim counter-truth looming up beyond, then weep not, but give thanks: It is the Lord's voice whispering 'Take Up Thy Bed and Walk.' " Living in the Truth means not being afraid of growth and change.

In spite of its multi-dimensional complexity, however, personal truth remains fundamentally simple. Jesus as the Living Truth is a symbol for absolute, simple *trust* in God's grace. As John Koenig, who teaches New Testament at General Episcopal Seminary in New York, wrote in a 1987 article, "Christ must be named so people can trust God through him." And this is not the kind of trust that makes Jesus into a lucky charm. It is simply childlike trust in the grace of God.

One of the most touching expressions of this trust is the wonderful gospel song, "His eye is on the sparrow, and I know he watches me." More than once Jesus is pictured as using the birds of the air to illustrate the experience of warm, personal trust in God. Oscar Hammerstein also captured this ethos of personal faith and trust in his lyrics relating to birds. In *South Pacific* he countered pessimism with the observation that "every whippoorwill is selling me a bill, and telling me it just ain't so." In his song "It's A Grand Night for Singing" he came up with this lovely line: "And somewhere a bird who is bound to be heard is throwing his heart at the sky!" What an absolutely marvelous way to describe the song of a bird, or any song for that matter — to "throw your heart at the sky"! What a marvelous way to personalize the universe which can sometimes appear to be cold and uncaring. To have simple faith and trust in God's grace is to throw our heart at the sky *and know that it will be caught*!

In his book about the dangers of fanatical cults, Howard J. Clinebell Jr. lists twelve tests for mentally healthy religion. The second item on his list reads, "Does a particular form of religious thought and practice strengthen or weaken a basic sense of trust and relatedness to the universe?" Healthy religion gives us a sense of personal belonging, of being at home in the world!

There is a bothersome contradiction in the attitude of some Christians who make an issue out of the necessity of believing literally in the physical resurrection of Jesus. The physical body of the historical Jesus and the physical reality of the empty tomb are treated like ultimate objects of veneration, and yet these same Christians often exhibit an overly spiritualized, otherworldly and "sex-negative" attitude in which physical bodies are denigrated. Such thinking affirms the physical world only in principle but not in reality and is, hence, disturbingly inconsistent. If we are going to affirm the personal and physical nature of the real, risen Jesus Christ, let us do it in a way that takes our own physical and personal experience seriously.

One way to do that is to care more about understanding each others' personalities than we do about winning theological arguments. If we really care about the down-to-earth personal nature of the Gospel of Jesus, we will take the time to read a book like *Please Understand Me* by David Keirsey and Marilyn Bates, in which we can learn how different personality types interact with one another. We might begin learning to get along much better with one another if we become aware of the fact that, for example, the personality-type of most clergy is quite different from the personality-type found among most parishoners. Most clergy are *Intuitives* (focusing on hunches, speculation, inspiration, fantasy, ingenuity and imagination), while most parishioners are *Sensates* (focusing on guidance from past experiences, realism, and down-to-earth practicality.) I know of a mother and son whose relationship was greatly improved when they learned to see many of their conflicts as resulting from differences in their personality-types rather than from deliberate attempts to get one another's goat.

The personal nature of Christian faith is also being promoted when a church journal publishes helpful articles like one in *The Lutheran*, June 3, 1987, which identified specific "storm signals for spouses." The article described weak points that can lead to big trouble unless the destructive patterns are altered.

So, faith in Jesus is personal and down-to-earth. It is a matter of the heart. But once again, finally, we must warn ourselves against believing too loudly. To speak of relating to God in a personal way is not the same thing as saying that God is "a person." When John's Gospel tells us that "God is a spirit, and they that worship him must worship him in spirit and in truth," we are not really being told definitively what God is. To call God "a spirit" is simply to say that God is more than a mere physical being. Describing God as "spirit" tells us much more about what God is *not* than about what God is. Who knows really what we mean by "spirit"? In the same way, when we speak of God as if God were a person, we really don't mean that God is a flesh and blood person with arms and legs like ours. To make such a claim would be to believe too loudly, would be to think more highly of our own notions than we ought. What we mean simply is that God "relates to us *in a personal way!*"

We can never truly comprehend God-language. I often refer to theology or "God-talk" as "the attempt to talk about the 'un-talk-about-able.' " (And most of us immediately recognize the wisdom of the aphorism which states that "a completely understood God is no God at all.") Whether we refer to God as He, She or It, is immaterial as long as we recognize the thrust of the Christian Gospel to be that a purely impersonal, mechanistic notion of God misses the heart of the matter. The heart of the matter is a matter of the heart. The real Jesus Christ symbolizes the Truth that "you've gotta have heart!"

Oscar Hammerstein personalized the image of the singing bird as "throwing his heart at the sky." Felix Mendelssohn wrote a wonderful Aria in his Oratorio *Elijah*, "Then Shall the Righteous Shine Forth Like the Sun In Their Heavenly Father's Realm." I have on occasion tried to restate the truth of this affirmation in somewhat less anthropomorphic terms by saying that it expresses "an upbeat attitude toward the mystery of existence." Ultimately, of course, whether we use more or less anthropomorphic language is not all that important. The important thing is that we open our hearts and minds to the reality of personal purpose and meaning in the world and in our lives — even if, as yet, we do not completely understand all the dimensions of that meaning and purpose. It is enough to know that life's meaning has to do with caring interpersonal relationships. It is enough to be able to throw our heart at the sky and say, "Smile! God loves you!"

John 10:22-30 (C,L)
John 10:27-30 (RC)

Easter 4

"Give Me Jesus"

I give them eternal life, and they shall never perish, and no one shall snatch them out of my hand.

(John 10:28)

I've seen it from both sides — from the side of the family with a difficult child and from the side of the mother who complained that one "rotten apple" in her son's third grade class was disrupting the learning environment for the whole group. Both sets of parents would no doubt prefer to live in a simple, unambiguous world in which everything rolled smoothly along like clockwork. The fact is, however, that even the best parents in the world cannot necessarily prevent their children from having emotional problems, and parents who are lucky enough to have relatively well-adjusted children cannot, and probably should not, totally insulate their children against disruptive influences in the environment. (You may have heard this, that children who are overprotected from contact with other children and with "the outside world" do not have the chance to develop many natural antibodies, and hence are more susceptible to infections and the like as they grow older. Perhaps we have a parable here that applies to other aspects of life as well.)

Colonel Oliver North became a household name and even somewhat of a folk hero because he tried to cut through the ambiguity of red tape and get things done. But his story has reminded all of us that a true democracy requires a complex system of checks and balances. Things may have seemed simpler in the days of yesteryear when the Lone Ranger "led the fight for law and order," but even then, vigilanteeism and self-righteous crusades were frowned upon. The Lone Ranger always turned things over to the local sheriff at an appropriate point.

There are people who won't even read a murder mystery novel or go to the movies because they want to avoid facing any of the harsh or ambiguous realities of life. To them it seems as if enjoying a TV show like "Murder, She Wrote" is tantamount to endorsing murder. The attitude is that we shouldn't even think about such things. Similarly, we can become upset at the notion of teaching drug users to use clean needles, as if to do so is to encourage drug abuse, when, in fact, the real purpose of this kind of educational effort is to prevent the problems of drug abuse from being compounded and made worse than they already are.

The point of all these observations is that we cannot hide from the complexity and ambiguity of life. We are in the process of considering the senses in which even our theology about Jesus is complicated and difficult. Our wintery story from John 10 again reminds us that people often have rough sledding in relationship to Jesus. A group with inquiring minds surrounds Jesus and wants to know in totally unambiguous terms if Jesus is the Christ: "How long will you keep us in suspense? If you are the Christ, tell us plainly." The answer given by Jesus is, in effect, that only unbelievers demand such unambiguous clarification. The observation that the Messiahship of Jesus is proclaimed only to his disciples and not to the general public is a way of saying that believers believe *in spite of the ambiguity*, not because all ambiguity has been explained away! "My sheep hear my voice, and I know them, and they follow me." On some profound level, the message of Jesus cuts through all ambiguity and goes straight to the heart. We are back to the theme of Jesus' hesitation to make grand claims about being the Christ. He would rather be seen as a lowly shepherd. Those who want him to pontificate with grand, clear and unambiguous claims are left disappointed.

Among those who still today want Jesus to prove conclusively that he is the Christ, there are a significant number of people and groups who insist that the accuracy of Bible predictions is the ultimate proof of his authenticity. But the word "prophecy" does not refer primarily to prediction. It basically means simply "to speak for someone else" — in the case of biblical prophecy it means to speak for God, on God's behalf. Secondly, sound biblical scholarship has demonstrated that many so-called predictions in the Bible are not actually predictions at all and that where biblical writers do use the element of prediction to validate their beliefs about Jesus they are using it more as an interpretive tool to show that their ideas are consistent with the tradition than as a proof! But above all we need to recognize that the demand for unambiguous proof is exactly what Jesus rejects many times, including when he says in our text "I told you, and you do not believe." Jesus is pictured over and over again as insisting that his message of the grace and love of God is self-validating and that we should not depend primarily on signs and proofs. The message itself, standing on its own, should be enough for us.

At least as early as Martin Luther's time the point was being made that not everything in the Bible is of equal importance. Luther's way of saying it was to insist that the value of any passage of Scripture was dependent upon the degree to which it illuminated the life and message of Jesus Christ. Many contemporary theologians have restated this point by saying that the one truly unique thing about the New Testament is its emphasis on the radical grace of God. This unique, self-validating, radical theology of grace both sets Christianity off from other religions and yet also makes possible a new openness for dialogue among the world's religions (as we discussed at some length during Lent). We have repeated many times that to focus on Jesus as the Christ is to focus on the Grace of God. It is this clear focus on God's unconditional love that cuts through all uncertainty and ambiguity, giving us a profound sense of belonging and security in the knowledge that the real Jesus Christ has arisen and lives in us.

Blessed assurance! Jesus is mine! (Fanny J. Crosby)

The story is told of a brilliant scientist at MIT. He was a leader in his field, but when it came to his religion he appeared to be a rather simple-minded biblical literalist. When asked why he refused to deal with the findings of scientific biblical scholars he would reply that "when it comes to my religion I want something completely different from the changing winds of scientific proof; I simply want to believe without question." I think we all realize that although a totally naive, blind faith is not to be admired, there is an element of truth in this scientist's attitude. At some point we simply must cut through all the uncertainty and ambiguity and *believe*! There is a sense in which we have to move from the theology *about* Jesus to the faith *of* and *in* Jesus.

One of the most moving expressions of this attitude that we may ever encounter is found in one of the (unfortunately) lesser-known Spirituals. The main theme of the song is: "And when I come to die, give me Jesus!" In other words, when push comes to shove, simple faith and trust in the grace of God is the bottom line. We cannot and should not ignore the complexity and ambiguity of faith and life, but there are times when we do cut through it all and get to bedrock.

In his book, *Future Shock*, Alvin Toffler explains how, in this modern world of rapid change, confusion and over-choice, we all need some kind of "stability zones" — regular habits, rituals, beliefs — whatever it is that gives us a stable point of reference. It would be difficult to deny the wisdom of Toffler's observation, or to miss its application to the role of religious faith in our lives. The grace of God as revealed in Jesus, the Christ, is surely our ultimate stability zone.

The great theologian, Paul Tillich, defined religion as "ultimate concern." When all the things that seem important to us — career, family, sex, money, patriotism, and the like — begin to pale in the face of eternal values, we realize that there is no substitute for religion. To go through life thinking that all these very good and important things are of ultimate concern, only to discover that they are not as important as we thought, could be compared to the feeling that people must have had at that moment on the quiz show "Let's Make A Deal" when they suddenly realized that they had chosen the wrong door. They could have had a prize worth thousands of dollars but instead they chose the door with the "booby present" behind it. What a sinking feeling to discover that we have put our ultimate trust in something that doesn't last, in something that is not worthy of our ultimate concern!

Sadly, the true spirit of what religion is about can also elude us if we are full of anger, rage, and a sense of hopelessness and powerlessness. An Islamic scholar appearing on a 1987 PBS program, stated that in many areas of the world the religion of Islam is a movement of the oppressed and dispossessed who feel that the secular state has failed them. The vehemence of some religious conviction is actually a desperate attempt to gain a sense of power or control over our life and the world. Many who "witness" for the Lord by presenting a carefully constructed theological system of Bible interpretation are actually just overcompensating for the fact that they feel angry, hopeless and powerless in the face of a confusing and apparently hostile world. Their religious system gives them back a feeling of power and control. Their dedication to winning others is more accurately seen as their desperate attempt to constantly reassure themselves that they are in control, that life is manageable. Religion as a source of power in this sense is not constructive. Our faith *does* properly act as a stability zone in the midst of a confusing and sometimes frightening world, but faith must not be fashioned into a billy club that we brandish in order to convince ourselves and others that we have authority, power, and control.

As cautious as we should be about an aggressive approach to evangelism that pushes people into "a decision for Christ," we can recognize in that kind of language a valid reminder of the need to keep our priorities straight. If by "making a decision for Christ" we mean a commitment to letting God be God in our lives, a commitment to remembering what really is the bottom line in life, then the talk of such a decision has its place. In Matthew's Gospel, Jesus reminds us to lay up treasures in heaven, "for where your treasure is, there will your heart be also." The playwrite Tennessee Williams put it another way: "Snatching the eternal out of the desperately fleeting is the great magic trick of human existence." But perhaps the Spiritual still says it best: "And when I come to die, *give me Jesus!*" Of course, Fanny Crosby's gospel song "Blessed Assurance! Jesus is mine!" also makes the same point beautifully (and the song made a wonderful backdrop for Sally Field's Academy Award winning movie, "Places in the Heart," a story that really struggles to clarify what life is all about).

Whether we stand at death's door or at the pearly gates, we need to be reminded over and over again what it *means* to have Jesus with us there. Use your imagination for a bit and contemplate what your speech will sound like at those pearly gates. Will it be something like: "Well . . . Golly . . . I did my best; I'm not perfect; I'm only human, but at least I usually tried to do good and certainly wasn't as bad as a lot of folks are. Please let me in." Or will it be: "Lord, Lord, I believed in your blood atonement and did everything I could to spread the word that anyone who didn't believe the same was lost!" Or, will your speech sound something like this: "Thanks, Lord, for not making my entrance into these gates dependent upon the adequacy of either my faith or my deeds. I know that even when I have managed to do my best it hasn't been good enough to make myself or the world perfect. No merit of my own I claim, but wholly lean on Jesus' name."

                *   *   *

"When I come to die, give me Jesus!" Give me the name that means "God will save." Give me the simple, blessed assurance that my destiny is in the hand of a loving and gracious God and that no one can snatch me out of that hand. Let me depart in peace. Open my heart to celebrate the grace of God which unites all things in Christ and moves toward a glorious and yet mysterious future — beyond our imagining!

John 13:31-35   Easter 5

Divine Liturgy, Divine Play, Divine Comedy

> *My dear children, I am only to be with you a little longer. You will seek me; (but) "Where I am going you cannot come." A new commandment I give to you, that you love one another; even as I have loved you . . ."*
>
> (John 13:33-34)

Has it occurred to you that in those parts of the United States where it comes on at 11:30 p.m., "Saturday Night Live" is also Sunday *Morning* Live? It might be good if we could bring a little more of the humor of that show with us to church on Sunday mornings. The skits on Saturday Night Live aren't always the greatest, but Sunday morning in church isn't always as lively as it should be either, so let's not throw stones. (Besides, now that so many folk have video recorders, we can usually find a way to watch the "Church Lady" and her various cohorts at another time and not feel that Saturday night is competing with Sunday morning.) What a wonderful job Dana Carvey does of keeping us church folks from taking ourselves too seriously! Together with cartoonists like Doug Marlette who gives us the comic strip "Kudzu," and Carvey's "Church Lady," satirists from Mark Twain to Mark Russell help us to see ourselves from refreshing and often enlightening new perspectives.

Marlette sparks renewed appreciation for familiar biblical texts — and reminds us that translation is as much an art as it is a science, when he gives us gems like this souped-up version of the Beatitudes: "Blessed are the bummed out, for they shall be mellowed . . . Blessed are the wimpy, for they shall inherit the whole nine yards . . . Blessed are they who are really into righteousness, for they shall pig out . . . Blessed are the squeaky clean, heartwise, for they shall check out the chief mucky-muck." And while the Rev. Will B. Dunn groans that he has had it with these new translations, he is not above a little friendly irreverence of his own. About to baptize a squealing child, he asks the parents to repeat the baby's name. "Upton Charles!" Are you sure you want to name him that? Do you realize what his friends will call him when he's a teenager? What? "Upchuck." With the bowl of baptismal water dripping over his head, the preacher laments "We should have gone over all that in the pre-baptismal counseling."

Slightly irreverent, without a doubt, but certainly not sacrilegious. The grace of God makes it possible for us to lighten up and develop a sense of humor. Some church calendars recognize this day as *Cantate* Sunday — a day to celebrate singing and music. Hence, it can also be a day to remind ourselves that the liturgy of the worship service is a kind of play or drama, and that, like the church organist, we can all "play the service," not taking it with the wrong kind of seriousness. Just as we have been learning not to take our physical and historical images of Jesus too seriously because Jesus is as much a symbolic figure as he is an historical person, so too we need to recognize that the liturgical drama of the church is a symbol. Jesus is a symbol for the themes of grace, hope, faith and love — and the liturgy is, therefore, a "symbol of a symbol." While the symbol may participate fully in that which it symbolizes, there is also a sense in which it is distinct from that which it represents. Jesus is the living embodiment of God's grace, but he is also distinct from God the Father. The Liturgy also embodies divine grace, but particular forms of worship are not to be *equated* with Jesus or God.

A few years ago one of the major denominational magazines featured on its cover an impressionistic portrayal of the suffering Jesus. Obviously thinking that the artist had produced something more like a betrayal of Jesus than a portrayal, one reader wrote to the editor: "What have you done to my dear, sweet Savior?" The Jesus portrayed in John 13:33 tells his disciples that they cannot and must not hold onto him too tightly. "I am only to be with you a little longer." Our desire to "have" Jesus just as *we* want him is a desire that must be resisted. John's theme is that Jesus is *gone away* and that we must learn to recognize and be open to ever new and changing forms of his presence with us.

As important and beautiful as an historically-accurate and artistic liturgy or mass may be, and although the Greek word from which we get "liturgy" refers to an act or *work* of religious ritual and service, we must resist the urge to take the "work" and forms of worship too seriously. Someone has dubbed folks who seem to be fanatics about liturgical practice "liturgiacs." The validity of a worship service (or worship "work") does not stand or fall with the way in which the presiding minister holds her hands during the eucharistic prayer! Of course, if one is using an historical liturgical form, one should not truncate or mangle that rite to the point where it is unrecognizable. If we want to be that free and creative, we should simply create a new form.

In some instances, our attitudes toward the "real presence" of Christ in the Sacrament of the Altar degenerate into an attempt to hold onto Jesus too tightly. Some of us hold the view that the bread and wine truly become the real presence of Christ to us only when we in fact partake of the physical elements. (Leftover or spilled wine, for instance, is simply wine. We should save or dispose of it with an appropriate sense of decorum, but not venerate it as if it were some kind of relic.) Ecumenical dialogue should proceed along the lines of placing the various doctrines about Christ's presence in the Eucharist on a continuum, with a strong doctrine of "transsubstantiation" at one extreme end, and an equally radical insistence that the bread and wine are *merely symbols* at the other end. When we do this I think it becomes apparent that we all really agree that the Sacraments involve *a unique combination of realism and symbolism!* It is not that Roman Catholic ideas of transsubstantiation are too "magical" or superstitious when they affirm the "real presence" of Christ in the Sacrament, or that Reformed ideas of the bread and wine as simply representing the presence of Christ are too vague and indefinite. The two views simply complement one another as we all struggle with the tension between our desire to "have" Jesus still with us and our realization that the New Testament reminds us not to hold onto Jesus too tightly.

The fact that Eastern Orthodox churches and the Western churches have long argued over when to celebrate some of the major festivals related to the life of Jesus, and the fact that we have a movable date for Easter, are further reminders to us that while Christians take history seriously, Christians also do not *confine* truth to historical facts. The movable date for Easter is a qualification of the "pure historicity" of Jesus and the Resurrection. The real Jesus Christ may be historical, but he is always for Christians something much more than merely historical! He is a Living Symbol for the grace and victory of God.

Neither life nor death shall ever from the Lord his children sever; Unto them his grace he showeth, And their sorrows all he knoweth."
(Caroline V. Sandell Berg)

In the story we have read today, from John, Jesus addresses the disciples as "Little children" or "Dear children." You may remember that he also calls them children in our text from two weeks ago. (John 21:5) And, of course, we all remember Luke's account of Jesus blessing the children and saying "Whoever does not receive the kingdom of God like a little child shall not enter it." (Luke 18:17) One of our loveliest hymns is the Swedish favorite, "Children of the heavenly Father." A major characteristic of children is their playfulness. We need to preserve a childlike, playful attitude toward the divine liturgy. Just as work and leisure go hand in hand to make us well-rounded human beings, and just as creating the world is both God's work and God's play, so too the divine liturgy (or work) can also be divine play.

The theater emerged in the Western church when highly-stylized plays or dramas based on biblical stories were created, often using free-wheeling imagination to fill in little details. For example, one of the earliest such plays focuses on the women going to the merchant and buying the spices and ointments they need to embalm the body of Jesus. In more ways than one, therefore, the divine liturgy is a form of divine play. The liturgies of the Eastern Orthodox churches tend to be quite long because they are essentially an acting out of the life of Jesus.

Most liturgies play around quite a bit with names, images and symbols for God. More often than not we begin "In the *name* of the Father, and of the Son, and of the Holy Spirit." It is fair to say that we are playing with the imagery of parent and child when we use this way of naming, of describing God. Surely we realize that these ways of describing God are inadequate symbols and that we should not take them too seriously. God may be *like* a Father or a Mother. Jesus may be *like* a Son, and we may be *like* children of God, but God is not bound by our human categories. We can play with anthropomorphic images but we must avoid the arrogance of creating God totally in *our* image. (Perhaps you have heard the joke that says "God created man in his image . . . and man returned the compliment!")

The great philosopher Plato, however, went to the opposite extreme of not valuing our human symbols and forms enough. He thought of everything in this world as nothing but a poor copy of the ideal thing (a chair, for example) in the mind of God. Since an actual chair is just a poor imitation of the "idea of chairness," it is not particularly valuable or important. For Plato, a *painting* of a chair was particularly useless and valueless because it was nothing but "an imitation of an imitation!" Plato had a very low opinion of art and artists because he felt that art was just too far removed from Reality. Plato would not have appreciated John's words about the glorification of Jesus as representing and symbolizing the glorification of God.

The Bible, on the other hand, greatly values symbols and artistic images because they remind us how much God cares about the material world and because they help to give us a broad-ranging perspective on truth. Playing around with various perspectives on life is a major part of what life is all about! This is what humor does also. One of the things that humor does for us is to give us a sense of distance from reality, making it easier for us to cope with painful and harsh realities at those times when we are in fact right up against them. In Latino cultures, people put death at arm's length by making fun of it with skeleton symbolism. We can laugh at the joke about the mausoleum being "a place for people who make ashes of themselves" (or other funeral and cemetery jokes) when death is not right at our doorstep, and then, when we are up against death for real, we have a balanced perspective which helps us cope better in the long run. We do the same thing when we sing "Neither life nor death shall ever from the Lord his children sever; unto them his grace he showeth, and their sorrows all he knoweth." Being aware of the grace of God, we can put sorrow, life, and death, in perspective — and cope with it much better in the long run. This is why we listen to sermons as well. We contemplate and examine all aspects of life even when they may not be of immediate concern, so that when we are faced with the inevitable problems, joys and sorrows of life we will be better prepared to deal with them.

Christian theology is not afraid to say that in a sense both Jesus and the Divine Liturgy present themselves to us as works of art. During the observation of the 25th anniversary of the death of Marilyn

Monroe, a commentator described how Marilyn went from being the historical Norma Jean to being a legend and ultimately a myth. To say that a person's life has taken on "mythic proportions" is to say that one's life has taken on levels of meaning far beyond the ordinary! The real Jesus Christ is a mythic being in this sense. The simple "Jesus of history" always stands in a healthy, dynamic and creative tension with the symbolic "Christ of faith."

The life of Jesus and the Divine Litury of the church give us many levels of meaning to play with. When John's Jesus says to the disciples, "Where I am going you cannot come," he is referring both to his going to death on the Cross and to his going into another dimension with God where there are "many mansions." It took time for these levels of meaning to sink in (especially, it seems, in the case of Peter, who, ironically, was to become the main leader of the church).

The liturgy of the Eucharist serves to remind us that "thanksgiving" in particular has many levels of meaning. Above all we are thankful for God's grace in Jesus, the Christ. We are grateful that our salvation depends on God and not on us. In all languages based on Latin, the word *grace* and the word *gratitude* are virtually synonymous. (In many languages the word for "thanks" sounds like the english word for grace — gratia, gracias, etc.) To be gracious is to show favor and unconditional love, and the only appropriate response to such grace is a spontaneous gratitude that spills over and becomes a channel of that grace to others. We love one another just as Jesus loves us.

Sadly, however, when many people say "thank you," they actually demonstrate their inability to receive a gift graciously. They feel that every favor must be returned. A "thank you" becomes a way of evening the score, of making sure that you haven't given me more than I have given you. There is nothing wrong with sharing favors and gifts in a spirit of mutual give and take, but we must also cultivate the ability to receive graciously when there is no way we can repay our benefactor. It may be more blessed to give than to receive, but we often find it most difficult to receive a gift graciously when we have no hope of returning the favor. Just as a performer must learn to accept a compliment graciously with a simple "thank you," unemcumbered by a heavy dose of false modesty, so too we can only accept God's grace like a gleeful child and go on our way rejoicing. (Incidentally, one ramification of what we are saying here about the various aspects of Christian thanksgiving is that it is not necessary to say "thank you" to the person who gives us the bread or wine during communion. The gift is from God, and the only gratitude God desires is a life in which we demonstrate the same kind of grace and loving service to others that we have seen demonstrated in the life of Jesus.)

One of ancient Israel's psalms of thanksgiving shows us what a short step it is from divine playfulness and graciousness to divine laughter and divine comedy. An appealing translation of Psalm 65:13 goes like this: "The valleys stand so thick with corn that they laugh and sing." Divine grace makes it possible for us to laugh and sing our way through life in spite of the fact that, as the joke goes, none of us will get out of here alive — in spite of the fact that everything we laugh about is also something we will probably cry about at one time or another. God's grace gives us a perspective like the perspective of a great comedian. The gift of faith is virtually identical with the gift of a sense of humor. Both give us that miraculous ability to maintain a positive attitude toward life no matter what happens. Both have to do with salvation — with healing. Both contribute to our physical and spiritual *health*.

Victor Borge's lampooning of classical music and musicians has brought great joy to many people over the years. A review of his 1987 San Francisco Pops performance concluded with these words: "A world without the gentle wit of Victor Borge would be a world diminished by the loss of graceful laughter." Since a sense of God's grace is the ultimate foundation for a sense of humor, maybe the title for this sermon should have been "Graceful Laughter." It's a great phrase so long as we don't equate "graceful" with "fainthearted." So if "Divine Liturgy, Divine Play, Divine Comedy" is too heavy for you — just remember to fill your life with *graceful laughter*.

John 14:23-29　　　　　　　　　　　　　　　　　　Easter 6

Becoming What Your Are

But the Counselor, the Holy Spirit, whom the Father will send in my name, he will teach you all things, and bring to your remembrance all that I have said to you.

(John 14:26)

If you have visited the Kremlin in Moscow, one of the things that probably sticks in your memory is the tomb of Lenin. I have heard visitors comment that the emphasis on tombs and monuments in the Soviet Union almost makes it seem as if the Soviet people worship cemeteries.

In contrast to being entombed and put on display like a specimen in a museum, Jesus tells his followers over and over again that he is going away. In John 14:28 he says, "I go away, and I will come to you." Jesus is pictured as deliberately going away and instructing his disciples to rejoice at his departure, because his physical absence will force them to focus on the new and changing ways in which he will continue to be a *living presence* among them. It is actually fortunate that to this day the exact sites of Jesus' birth, baptism, crucifixion and tomb remain a matter of conjecture. The sites shown to tourists in Bethlehem and Jerusalem simply cannot be authoritatively verified as authentic. Although some churches — especially famous cathedrals — have become as much museums (and in some cases even mausoleums) as churches, Christians do not think of their church buildings as monuments to "the late, departed Jesus." The real church consists of the people who love what Jesus stands for. To use Saint Paul's imagery, the people who create the church buildings are themselves the real body of Christ. The real Jesus Christ is the Jesus whose story comes alive as it is retold in countless creative ways — through preaching and the Sacraments, through the arts, through active involvement in social issues where the true meaning of love is acted out by those who love the world and its people as much as God does.

If you have noticed that pastors often seem to dislike funeral chapels, you should know that the cause of the apparent anomosity is not professional jealousy. The mortuary funeral chapel is used for only one purpose and is associated with nothing but death. The church building, on the other hand, is associated with all aspects of life. All kinds of things go on at churches — baptisms, weddings, potlucks, many types of meetings, day care, choir rehearsals, funerals, worship services, confirmations. Churches are associated with life in all its variety and splendor, in all its sorrow and pain. The church reminds us that the story of Jesus is more about life than about death.

John's Gospel tells us that Jesus will continue to be a living presence among us as a "Counselor" and as "the Holy Spirit." This counseling Spirit has two primary roles: (1) to remind us of what Jesus has already said about abiding in his love, and (2) to teach us everything that we need to know as we move into the future (in the words of John 16:12, to "lead us into all the truth.") The clear implication of this twofold role is that while our own positive self-esteem is *already* established through the knowledge that we are unconditionally loved and valued by God, that while we *already* have that peace which the world cannot give, that while we *already* are saved and justified, or, to put it more dramatically, that while we *already* are *saints* — we are still in the process of *becoming* righteous, of *becoming* people who love as much as God loves, of *becoming* saints. In traditional theological terms the work of the Holy Spirit is called Sanctification and the work of Jesus is called Justification. Through justification by grace, God sees us as already restored to the image that we were meant to have — God sees us as already saints. Yet the doctrine of Sanctification reminds us that much remains to be done. Sanctification is the process of *"becoming* what we already *are."* The Holy Spirit is, among other things, a Symbol for *moving ahead*, a Symbol of *becoming*, a Symbol for the *process* of moving into the future.

It's not hard to understand why a lot of us are uncomfortable with the label "saint." The term earns some negative connotations — such as holier-than-thou, or goody-two-shoes, or fanatic. But to insist that we are neither saints nor sinners, that we are "only human," is to miss the wonderful paradox in the idea that we are to become what we already are. To be a saint in the Christian sense is to be humble and human "to the max," but at the same time it is to have the wonderfully reassuring confidence that God does much more than simply reward or punish us according to our deserts. God makes it possible for us, as we have often repeated, to combine a sense of urgency about being all that we can be, with a sense of humor that doesn't take our efforts at perfection too seriously. The mathematician and philosopher Blaise Pascal expressed this marvelously humble sense of confidence and trust in God's ability to make us into the saints that we could never become on our own, when he said, "I would not be searching for God unless God had already found me."

In the last few years we have all had to get used to the more accurate transliteration of the name for God in the Hebrew Scriptures. That name, Yahweh, is based on the same letters that form the basic verb "to be" in the Hebrew language. In the familiar story of the burning bush, Moses is pictured as asking what God's name is, and the voice from the bush answers with a booming *"I am."* Scholars have been intently studying this interesting name for God, and many are convinced that a more accurate translation of its meaning would be *"I will become who I will become."* This forward-moving, future-oriented name fits in remarkably well with the description of the Holy Spirit as the one who leads us forward into all the truth. It suggests that all of life is a process of becoming, of creating, of growing in grace and love.

Another famous mathematician and philosopher, Alfred North Whitehead, developed his entire philosophical system around this concept of becoming. His "Process Philosophy" has inspired the development of a process *theology* that begins by defining God as "the never-ending source of novelty." While in a sense this is just a fancy way of describing God as Creator, it does bring in more clearly the element of forward motion, of ongoing development, change and growth. Life is seen as a process of becoming! The controversial French Jesuit priest and scientist, Pierre Teilhard de Chardin, liked to observe that in addition to describing God as beyond and above us, we should also think of God as being *ahead of us*!

Your kingdom come, O God . . . Where is your reign of peace And purity and love? When shall all hatred cease, As in the realms above?
(Lewis Hensley)

This hymn expresses an almost impertinent impatience over the apparent slowness of the process whereby the world is becoming what God intends it to be. Instead of the phrase "as slow as molasses in January," some folks use the expression "as slow as the second coming of Christ." Let's look at some of the ramifications of this emphasis on the theology of becoming, the theology of process, the theology of the Spirit. Is the Kingdom coming too slowly, or are we looking for the wrong things?

Let's return to the doctrine of Sanctification as expressed in the statement "You are a saint . . . now become what you are." The great Russian author Dostoevsky wrote, "One can love one's neighbor in the abstract or even at a distance. But at close quarters, it's almost impossible!" To say that we already are saints and that now our job is to become what we are, is to say that we should put abstract notions of perfection behind us, relax, and concentrate on simply becoming as fully human as possible. God will take care of the big picture. The ultimate, "abstract," questions having to do with justice, salvation, perfection and the like can only be answered or solved by God. We are freed to concentrate on the concrete, everyday, down-to-earth, often nitty-gritty job of loving our neighbors "at close quarters."

To say that we are saints in the process of becoming what we are is in part just another way of making the traditional point that Christians see themselves to be both sinners and saints at the same time. Of course, we have all heard people make fun of this image of sinner-saints by saying that Christians go to church and get forgiveness and then go right out and do the same sins all over again . . . and again . . . and again. Saint Paul himself had to deal with this issue in his letter to the Romans. He asked the rhetorical question, "Are we to sin all the more so that grace may abound?" The question came up because the anti-legalistic tone of the Christian faith did indeed sometimes make it *seem* as if Christians were rather lax in their attitude toward the law — and, in fact, some followers of "The Way," as members of the early church were called, *did* espouse a cavalier disregard for ethics. It has been necessary for Christians to be constantly on guard against misunderstandings that can arise over the meaning of their new attitude toward the law and ethics.

As important as laws and ethical principles are, the basic Christian insights are that (1) laws must never become straight-jackets for us, and (2) we do not achieve perfection by a slavish obedience to law. The purpose of law is to remind us that an abstract notion of perfection is unattainable by one's own efforts, but at the same time to remind us that we should keep *moving in the right direction*!

By expressing our sense of longing for the time when peace and love will reign, when hatred and wars shall cease, the hymn makes it crystal clear that life is a process of moving toward goals. Ethical standards and utopian visions help us to move in the right direction, but if we take them too seriously and too literally they can do more harm than good. Our goal is not some static and abstract notion of perfection or peace. That is the kind of peace that the world may give, but it is not the kind of peace offered by Jesus. Our goal is to continue the process of living. The peace offered by Jesus has to do with life, with the never-ending process of *becoming*.

In a sermon titled "A New Vision," Dr. E. Howard Satterwhite of Trinity United Methodist Church in Alexandria, Virginia, compared the ideal of a Christian community of love, with a marriage in which the romance has faded, the honeymoon is over, and the relationship has become a labor of love requiring simple tenacity, "hanging in there." Describing his vision of Christian love at close quarters he said, "We should lose the illusions of perfection . . . if we are looking for perfection here, we had better go somewhere else. But no one else has it either. We need to deal with the fact that we are imperfect and yet are in love as community. The community cannot save us from anything and we cannot save anyone else, not on our own skills and not on our charms. But trusting in God we become more trustworthy to each other, and more available for the authentic community that is grounded in God's power and not our own."

We are not perfect. We are not know-it-alls. We are merely becoming. But our hearts are not troubled by this "not yet" aspect of faith in Jesus. Dr. Leslie Weatherhead, prolific author and for close to 30 years minister at the famous Methodist City Temple of London, wrote that "any minister, standing in the pulpit, who is not an agnostic, is dangerous." His point was that healthy religion encourages us to foster our inquisitive spirit, to avoid giving the impression that we have final and absolute answers, and to leave salvation and perfection in God's hands. I would add that Weatherhead's notion of "the Christian agnostic" is a simple reminder to us to be always humble about our God-talk! To some degree, whether one uses the label atheist, agnostic or theist is not all that important. God-talk should always be a humble attempt to carry on the most *profound* discussion of life possible in the *broadest* possible context. It is the attempt to talk about "the un-talk-about-able." Just as I always want to discuss what it *means* to believe in Jesus, I would rather take the time to discuss with someone what it *means* to believe in God than to simply answer the question of whether or not I believe in God with a flat yes or no. God will be what God will be regardless of our doctrines and pet notions. To believe in God is perhaps above all to be humble — and human.

The book of Genesis tells us that as human beings we are made in the divine image. God's name means "I will become who I will become." To believe in God, to see oneself as made in God's image and as one of God's beloved saints, is not in the least bit arrogant or self-agrandizing. It is simply to embrace with confidence (with faith) the exciting process of becoming what you are!

Luke 24:44-53   Ascension Day/Ascension Sunday

Jesus Meets Buddha and Confucius

> *It is written that the Christ should suffer and on the third day rise from the dead, and that repentance and forgiveness of sins should be preached in his name to all nations . . .*
>
>   (Luke 24:46-47)

Are you familiar with the book called "The Lost Years of Jesus"? The popularity of this book — which has also inspired a movie — indicates that many people have become fascinated with the idea that Jesus went off to India before his ministry began in Palestine. One version of the story has it that Jesus appeared in the form of a great Indian guru. Another approach suggests that Jesus and Buddha were actually the same divine being appearing in different forms. In 1977, Harvey Cox, a professor at Harvard Divinity School, published his excellent book *Turning East*, in which he discussed various aspects of the Western fascination with Eastern religion and philosophy.

While the desire to believe that Jesus somehow is connected with other great religious figures like Buddha and Confucius is totally understandable, we must not let our desire to foster unity among the various religious traditions of the world blind us to the fact that there are extremely important differences between these traditions. In order to promote true unity and understanding among all nations and religions, we must pay as much attention to the salient differences between these faiths as to the exciting similarities. We do not create unity between Jesus, Buddha and others, by riding roughshod over history.

We have noted many times that the stories of Jesus reflect a paradoxical attitude toward history. On the one hand, just preceeding our text from Luke chapter 24, we read of the incident where the risen Jesus eats a fish to demonstrate that he is not simply a disembodied ghost. Luke is concerned to point out that he takes the physical world, and history, seriously. Yet, on the other hand, at the very end of his Gospel and our text (and in his continuation of the story in the book of Acts), Luke pictures Jesus as more or less vanishing into thin air as he ascends into heaven. It does make some sense that if Jesus is able to vanish into thin air at the conclusion of his ministry, he could also have used astral projection or some form of "soul travel" during the early years of his life not recorded by the evangelists, in order to make contact with other parts of the world — in order to meet Buddha, Confucius, Mohammed and others.

But Luke begins the episode we have read today by setting Jesus firmly in the specific historical context of Moses, the laws, the hymns, and the prophets of Israel! He shows Jesus offering to his disciples a specific interpretation of the uniquely Jewish concept of the Messiah, the Christ. It is not so much that historical events *prove* spiritual truths, or that Moses and the prophets are important because they *predicted* what Jesus would do — it is rather that the Christian faith simply takes history seriously enough to insist that we must not ignore the specific historical and cultural settings in which religious teachings arise. The real Jesus is the Jesus who embodies a particular interpretation of the Christ (the Messiah) as one who suffers, defeats death, and offers forgiveness of sins.

One of the fundamental differences between the so-called Western religions like Judaism and Christianity, and the Eastern religions like Hinduism and Buddhism, is that in the Western faiths we are saved from *sin*, whereas in the Eastern faiths we are saved from *ignorance*. The Western religions are usually described as "ethical-historical monotheisms," where the emphasis is on ethical behavior in the day-to-day affairs of life. The Eastern religions are, by contrast, religions of "cosmic, monistic consciousness." Their emphasis is more on knowledge than on ethics. The assumption is made that once we have clear knowledge of the spiritual oneness of all and the unreality of the material world, then ethical actions — to the degree that they matter — will automatically follow.

The main issue for Christianity, however, is that even when we know what is true and right, we often don't act accordingly. There is a problem with our will, our sinful impulses. Enlightenment alone is not enough.

The tendency to emphasize knowledge crept into the Christian tradition in the form of Gnosticism. The greek word, *gnosis*, means knowledge, and early on, the Christian church rejected the interpretation of Jesus as a Messiah whose main project was to bring saving *knowledge*. What is to be preached in the name of Jesus is not knowledge, but love and *forgiveness of sins*! "Repentance" is a change of mind not toward an abstract notion of cosmic consciousness but a change of mind that affects our everyday behavior in relationship to others. The grace of God as seen in Jesus is directed primarily toward helping us face the ethical challenge of promoting righteousness and justice, without falling into despair over the Herculean proportions of the task — whereas the grace of God as understood by Buddha is directed primarily at giving us mental clarity, cosmic consciousness, cosmic enlightenment (the name Buddha means "awakened" or "enlightened").

None of this is to say that Buddha is Buddha and Jesus is Jesus and never the twain shall meet. Buddhism is indeed concerned about ethical issues and Christianity is also concerned about intellectual and spiritual knowledge. But to pretend that Jesus and Buddha, that Christianity and Buddhism are essentially the same, is simplistic at best, and historically, theologically, and culturally dishonest at worst. The Jesus pictured by all the New Testament writers deals with a whole different set of issues than does the Buddha who in his own unique, historical context developed and reformed the beliefs of Hinduism.

A hymn of glory let us sing! New hymns throughout the world shall ring: Alleluia! Christ, by a road before untrod, Ascends unto the throne of God. (The Venerable Bede)

The proper way for Jesus and Buddha to meet is for those of us who represent these traditions today to enter into dialogue over the similarities and differences in our approaches to faith. Due in part to the writings and work of Shirley MacLaine, one of the growing issues that we need to discuss is the phenomenon known as trance channeling. The basic idea is that disembodied souls or spirit guides can communicate with us "from the other side," giving us knowledge of spiritual truths. Believers in trance channeling tend to suggest that Jesus himself was very much like one of these spirit guides. The problem (and point for dialogue) is that this concept of spirit guides is based on the specifically Eastern notion that mind or consciousness is *more real* than physical or historical reality, while the Christian tendency is to affirm — in a deliberately paradoxical way — that both the spiritual and physical worlds are equally real and important. In the texts relating to the resurrection appearances and the ascension of Jesus, there is a constant, unresolved tension between describing them as bodily events and as spiritual events. To describe Jesus, therefore, as simply a divine entity who could flit about at will to India or appear in various forms as Buddha, as Jesus, as Mohammed . . . is not so much for Jesus to *meet* Buddha as for Jesus to surrender his identity to Buddha, to become just another "enlightened one," just another spiritual guide among many.

In other words, when Jesus is defined so completely in terms of the Buddhist worldview, Jesus ceases to exist as a unique, historical symbol, *as the very thing that the New Testament writers clearly want him to be*! Jesus may be more than an historical figure, but the stories about him are clearly and deliberately set in a particular historical context. Tha ascension hymn attributed to The Venerable Bede, who lived around A.D. 700, emphasizes the *unique identity and role of Jesus* by using the poetic image of Christ ascending ". . . by a road before untrod." We do not hinder religious unity by being honest about the *uniqueness* of Jesus, of Buddha, of Confucius.

Buddhist-Christian dialogue can be extremely helpful in clarifying issues *within* the Christian community. In 1980 a major theological journal devoted an entire issue to the topic of "Lutherans in Crisis over Justification by Faith." One of the points made was that the emphasis of the charismatic and pentecostal movements upon the subjective experience of "feeling the spirit" is in danger of transforming Christian faith into a Buddhist-style emphasis on spiritual knowledge, at the expense of the ethical concerns embodied in the doctrine of justification by grace through faith. In other words, Christianity is always tempted to give up its distinctive contribution to theology — the radical notion of grace as the unconditional love of God for sinners, which motivates them to do their best in an urgent yet relaxed frame of mind — and to exchange it for a more general or typical notion of "spiritual knowledge" and "spiritual feelings." Christians are tempted to enter the business of channeling esoteric knowledge (whether through spiritual entities or not is "immaterial," pun intended), and to give up on channeling grace.

This issue of the role of ethics in religion is probably the single most important point of discussion between Buddhists and Christians. Take, for example, the currently popular subject of so-called "New Age Higher Consciousness." New age awareness of the "higher self" can easily turn into a selfish preoccupation with our own ego. But instead of being an excuse for self-absorption, the search for our higher self can encourage us to find ourselves by relating to and caring about others. We can learn the difference between being self-centered and being a centered self, between selfishness and true self-love. One of the beauties of Buddhism is its doctrine of the "Middle Path," which advises us to find ourselves somewhere between the extremes of self-indulgence and self-denial.

Many people who come for pastoral counseling need more than anything else to become engaged with the world outside of themselves — to care about someone else, to get a job or make a commitment that gives them less time to worry about their personal problems and hang-ups. My grandmother understood this. She had many problems of her own, but she surmounted them by helping others and concentrating on their needs. She especially enjoyed visiting lonely shut-ins.

We discussed reincarnation on Easter Sunday, but since, together with the doctrine of Karma, the logic of reincarnation is the primary key to understanding the Buddhist/Hindu attitude toward ethics, we need to look at a few more angles on what the Indians call Karma-Samsara. One of the main appeals of this twin doctrine is that it offers to explain how life is always fair in the long run. The problem with this concept of the relationship between the "now" and the "not yet," from the Judeo-Christian perspective, is that it is too patient. By maintaining that we have virtually endless time and infinite, multiple identies through which we can work out our karma, reincarnational thinking encourages a relatively *laissez faire* or detached attitude toward issues of social justice and ethics. In contrast, the Christian attitude is characterized by a certain impatience, as illustrated by a cartoon I saw recently in which a little guy is looking up to heaven and saying, "Er . . . in case you haven't noticed . . . the meek are still getting creamed down here . . ." As we have noted many times, the whole point of the Christian emphasis on grace is to keep us from giving in to despair as we struggle to make ourselves and the world all that it is meant to be.

Perhaps the greatest *danger* of reincarnational logic is the impression it gives that we deserve everything we experience in this life. If karma is the reason for everything that happens, then we must accept our fate without objection or resistance. The danger is that we will become "moralistic" and, for example, blame people who become sick, saying they have done wrong or have not developed enough spiritual consciousness to transcend disease. When *Newsweek* did its issue on "The Faces of AIDS," it quoted James Hurley, an AIDS sufferer: "There's no such thing as being an innocent or guilty victim of AIDS. That anyone has this disease is a tragedy." Diseases like AIDS remind us of the dangers of moralizing and judgmentalism. The issue must never become one of fairness — of explaining how we deserve our fate — but rather one of identifying with suffering and struggling to overcome it.

Taking language about the Devil literally may seem to be a way of dealing seriously with the reality of evil, but like the doctrine of Karma-Samsara, it tends to make us moralistic rather than ethical. We can get so wrapped up in being appalled over satanic lyrics in heavy metal rock music, for example, that we miss the real issues involved — many having to do with adolescent psychology. The music may be nothing more than an expression of the typical adolescent need to begin the process of establishing independence from ones parents (often by deliberately trying to shock them). This process has become more and more difficult in our society, which, for educational and other reasons, encourages "prolonged adolescence." Or for some people this type of music may be simply a way of blowing off steam. (Remember the tongue-in-cheek song "Fie on Goodness!" from *Camelot*?) For still others, an interest in satanic lyrics or movies that glorify the occult and horror, may indicate psychological problems: a poor self-image, low self-esteem, or (a subtle but major problem with many troubled young people) a fear of success. (Yes . . . some people are so accustomed to failure that the prospect of doing well frightens them into deliberate sabotage of their efforts, and into outrageous glorification of everything perceived as negative and destructive!)

The overall point is that just as movies like *The Exorcist* can distract us (with a lot of literalistic, satanic mumbo-jumbo) from the real ethical issues in our society, so too, religion that puts more emphasis on knowledge/mind/consciousness than on ethics can lead us down the primrose path of escapism, detachment and moralism. While this criticism may sound harsh, it must be remembered that since believing in Jesus means to believe that the salvation of "all nations" is in God's hands, such criticism in no way implies that non-Christian religions are worthless and false. The criticism is intended only to foster dialogue.

We haven't said much about the religions of the Far East, but it is also important to carry on a dialogue between Jesus and Confucius. The Chinese concept of the Tao provides us with many valuable insights. It reminds us eloquently that our efforts to define God are necessarily inadequate. It recognizes the paradoxical nature of life — especially the paradox of faith as something both to be actively achieved (yin) and passively received (yang). And it emphasizes the importance of being involved in the community of humankind, in society.

The problematic element in Confucianism is that it fosters such total reverence for cultural community and traditions that ethics is reduced to little more than etiquette! Moses and the prophets were able to criticize even the most popular opinions or officials of their day on the basis of ethical principles that transcended mere cultural prejudices. It remained for Lao Tzu, the founder of Taoism, to make this kind of ethical thought and critisim legitimate in China.

Narrow-minded, culturally biased moralism — often masquerading under the guise of "common sense" — frequently produces the opposite of ethics. It can cause a lot of injustice and pain. In our own society I think of people who are embarrassed about medical procedures simply because of the parts of the body involved. They act as if it is virtually sinful to have certain diseases or medical problems when, in fact, the whole situation is morally neutral. I think in particular of a young man like Saul Lubaroff who suffers from Tourette's syndrome, a strange disease that causes a person to go into uncontrollable spasms of shouting obscenities and insults. How many folks will moralistically rush to judgment when they encounter Saul? I think also of the down-to-earth hard work done by skilled psychiatric social workers to rehabilitate emotionally disturbed children. They have remarkable success precisely because they avoid naive moralizing and instead help children to work through their feelings. Once the child begins to understand his or her feelings, then behavior usually improves.

Another example of the way in which moralistic attitudes are counterproductive to ethical intentions is provided in this letter to the editor of *The Lutheran* magazine: "I am concerned about the decision (of the Bishops) requiring pastors upon divorce to express intent or willingness to resign. I am clergy, and I am divorced. Through nine months of marital therapy my former wife and I discovered we are best friends, but for us it wasn't enough to sustain a ten-year marriage. We were completely open with my congregation . . . After the divorce my relationship with my parishioners deepened. They then were able to tell me their own troubles more easily. To suggest resignation from the parish and possible removal from the clergy roll to divorcing clergy doesn't speak well of the capacity for mutual ministry in the parish. This also would cloud any marital therapy process. With one's job at stake in addition to one's marriage, decision-reaching is more difficult, and what should happen may not."

Instead of shallow moralism, the real Jesus comes to us with a message of morality under grace. He symbolizes the ongoing process of struggling with ethics and social issues. He teaches us to reject what someone once called "the stupid game of 'Bible Land' " in which we naively model our ethical judgments on what happened to characters in the Bible. Rather than simply trying to mimic the cultural mores of Bible times, we are set free by grace to "do ethics," to struggle with ethical issues as Jesus did — maintaining a sense of humor (*not* of passive detachment!), and using the Scriptures for guidance but not as a straightjacket. In so doing, we continue to be channels of God's grace.

John 17:20-26　　　　　　　　　　　　　　　　　　Easter 7

The Real Jesus is Channeling Grace

> *I made known to them your name, and I will make it known, that the love with which you have loved me may be in them, and I in them.*
>
> (John 17:26)

Over the last couple decades we have heard critics decry what has been variously described as "civil religion," "religion in general," or "the religion of the American way of life." Recently, Dr. Robert Jenson, a professor at Lutheran Theological Seminary in Gettysburg, Pennsylvania, restated the criticism this way: "The God proclaimed in American Protestantism is inoffensive — a God who makes no difference . . . mainline Protestantism is to a great extent atheistic."

I think Dr. Jenson and the other critics are onto something, but I would like to state the issue a little differently. The real problem is not that we are becoming atheistic but that we are becoming *a-theological*! In the name of ending divisiveness and promoting unity we have tended to shy away from talking about doctrines and theological dogma. It's not that we have become thoroughly atheistic but that we are hesitant to talk about what believing in God means. At one extreme we have those who retreat blindly into traditional dogmatism, claiming that everyone must accept their particular version of believing in God . . . and, at the other extreme, we have the tendency to reduce religion to a bland, moralistic blend of cliches, pop psychology, pop sociology and (sometimes) media hype. A recent *TV Guide* advertisement for Robert Schuller's "Hour of Power" promoted this series of messages: "Six Success Points for Parents," "Ten Tips for Teens," and "Eight Words of Wisdom for Husbands and Wives." No doubt there was much helpful material in these presentations, but they clearly illustrate the phenomenon of "a-theological Christianity."

We do not make religion more palatable and meaningful to people by diluting the message or by avoiding God-talk! We do not promote religious unity by homogenizing all religious ideas and reducing them to their lowest common denominator. What we need to do is to work with our classical theological traditions and discover anew how they relate to our own day and age! We have been doing just that as we have asked what it *means* to believe in Jesus, what it *means* to use "God-talk." Jesus says in our text that he has made God's name known and will make it known in the future. His words are being fulfilled as we continue to study what the names "Jesus" and "God" mean for us today.

Of course, what we have discovered, and what our text for today drives home, is that the name *Jesus* means "God will save" and that, therefore, the grace of God and the grace of Jesus are one and the same! John's version of Jesus' lengthy prayer for the unity of all ends with Jesus saying "that the love with which you have loved me may be in them, and I in them." This unifying, unconditional love, this agape, is the grace that the real Jesus channels to us all, which in turn makes us into channels of the same grace and love to others. The doctrine of grace does not build walls between people. It is the kind of theology that breaks down barriers and results in the most profound kind of unity possible. John pictures the unity of Jesus and God, in love, as a model for all of us to follow.

Professor Jenson says that the God proclaimed by American Protestant religion in general is "inoffensive." To the degree that such religion is bland, naively moralistic and a-theological (*non*-theological), we could perhaps agree with his assessment. But if his objection is that a theology based on grace and love is too "soft," too positive in tone, too easy-going — then we must wonder whether his real concern is to stand up for the Gospel. The Gospel of Jesus Christ *does* challenge us, but the Christian message does not try to be offensive just for the sake of being offensive. The fact is that while John the evangelist views "the world" *both* as hostile to Jesus *and* as the object of God's love, the overall focus is upon God's love for the world. The overall tone is positive. The theme of judgment against the world is clearly secondary. The message of Jesus is not intended to create a small, cliquish in-group of people who don't want to have anything to do with the world. The grace and love of God in Christ makes it possible for the world community to know and believe in unity and peace.

Of course, to the degree that this is a success-mad and merciless world in which many things are wrong, the world needs to face judgment. But God's desire is to convert the world, not to condemn or destroy it. God loves the world! (Remember John 3:16.)

The Church's one foundation Is Jesus Christ, her Lord . . . One holy name she blesses . . . Lord, save us by your grace. (Samuel J. Stone)

When Jesus says "I do not pray for these only, but also for those who believe in me through their word, that they may all be one," he is recognizing that the extension of the church, the "inclusive ministry" of the church, may threaten its unity. It was sad to see the great hymn celebrating Jesus Christ as the Church's one foundation, being sung as a rallying point for those who felt forced out of the Lutheran Church — Missouri Synod because of doctrinal and other conflicts. Many of the apparent divisions within the Christian Church are more accurately seen simply as expressions of the healthy diversity of the church. But, unfortunately, a sizable number of these divisions are also disturbing evidence of a lack of unity and understanding among Christians — and many non-Christians are very much turned off by this lack of unity, this in-fighting.

Using the imagery of many different flocks of sheep in one sheepfold, of many mansions (or rooms) in his Father's house, the Jesus we meet in John's Gospel makes it clear that unity does not necessarily mean uniformity. Unity among people always has to be a "unity amid diversity." In speaking to the Lutheran Church — Missouri Synod convention during the LCMS schism, Bishop David Preus of the American Lutheran Church gently chided the delegates, saying that while some people seem to view the church as a loaf of white bread, he preferred to think of the church as more like a fruitcake, where there is always room for a few nuts! The point is that the followers of Jesus should always be expanding their notion of what unity means.

The recently-coined term "inclusive ministry" challenges us to join together under the grace of God to celebrate our diversity in ethnic backgrounds, lifestyles, theological traditions, and a host of other areas. Rather than making demands and claims upon one another in the name of Christ, we need to learn from the young Roman Catholic priest suffering with AIDS who said in a newspaper interview, "I have learned that the power of the Cross came from the fact that when Jesus hung there he was totally vulnerable, totally powerless. And he was so powerless in human terms that he became irresistable and drew the whole world for all time to come to the foot of that cross . . . The more vulnerable I become because of AIDS, because of my willingness to tell the truth about my life and who I am, the more I can be available to love."

Jesus is an appealing and unifying figure because he is vulnerable and "full of grace," not because he makes arrogant claims.

Some observers have said that the recent mess in the "evangelism business" has hurt the overall Christian witness. Others have noted that as media ministries parade their failings and weaknesses before the public, more people will be drawn to the less glamorous but more real community to be found in local congregations. Be that as it may, there can be little doubt that infighting among those who claim to be Christians is offensive to the world, and that this is not the kind of positive offensiveness Dr. Jenson has in mind — the offense of challenging all people to review their priorities and commitments. No. The world is legitimately horrified and repulsed when it sees Christians failing to live up to their own message of unity, love and understanding. In May of 1987 a number of major newspapers carried a cartoon showing the emperor Caesar in his box seat at the coliseum. He is telling his centurian, "Hold the lions. The Christians are eating each other, looks like."

The church is intended to be a model of how unity works. It is to show the world how we can all live together in peace despite our many differences. Christ is a symbol of our common humanity under God's love and grace. As Christians we must begin to polarize less, and dialogue more *among ourselves* so that Jesus' prayer for unity may be answered. Instead of dismissing each other with labels like "liberal," "conservative," "simplistic literalist" or "secular humanist," let us take each other seriously and talk together, trying to understand one another.

You might want to object and say that Jesus didn't tell us to "Go, therefore, and 'have dialogue' with all nations," but to "make disciples." True. But in this commission from Matthew's Gospel, "making disciples" is explicitly defined in terms of teaching all nations about the love and grace of God. And the best way for us to do that is to engage the world and our own various "communions" in dialogue — *theological* dialogue!

If you have seen the academy award winning film *Ghandi*, you may remember the scene where Ghandi is caught in the middle of intense conflict between Muslims and Hindus. He defuses the situation by saying "I am a Muslim, and a Hindu, and a Christian, and a Jew." This is a wonderful attitude to take, so long as it affirms the unique identities and contributions of each tradition, so long as it is a recognition of unity amid diversity rather than of superficial homogenizing of the various faiths. As we noted on Ash Wednesday, Christians in particular may need to begin paying more serious attention to the other major religions of the world. Many folks are so ignorant of anything beyond the Judeo-Christian tradition that when they do run into another faith-system they are immediately swept off their feet and become infatuated.

In the name of understanding and unity based on the grace of God, we surely need to avoid the attitude expressed by a group of parents who wanted *The Diary of Anne Frank* banned from the classroom because it seemed to approve of all religions without recognizing the superiority of Christianity. Ghandi's sentiment is a great antidote to such, no doubt well-intentioned holier-than-thou-ism. The Charlton Heston movie *El Cid* (which means "The Lord") illustrated both the horrible destructiveness of religious conflicts and the possibilities for overcoming religious-based hostility. The story of El Cid illustrates how the desire to win or claim other people for one's faith can become a prescription for cruel tyranny. Faith is shared through humble dialogue and by loving interaction, not by making claims and demands.

The relatively new faith called Bahai has looked promising to many people because it seems to have developed out of a desire to bring unity among all the religions of the world. But, unfortunately, instead of simply focusing on the great insights of all these religions, Bahai has gone in the direction of promoting its own unique ideas and organization as "The answer" to the question of religious and world unity. The problem is that whenever a group is formed to be the ultimate and final answer, it only succeeds in becoming just one more group vying for prominence among many others. Instead of leading to unity it merely adds one more voice to an already complex and confusing cacophony of claims and counter-claims.

Despairing of the possibility of ever bringing about religious unity through doctrinal, philosophical or theological dialogue, a great many people have latched onto the Golden Rule as the ultimate expression of their faith. It is provocative and inspiring to discover the remarkable universality of this ethical principle. In Hinduism it is stated like this: "Those gifted with intelligence should always treat others as they themselves wish to be treated." The Shinto version is: "The suffering of others is my suffering; the good of others is my good." In Buddhism it is: "A person can minister to friends and familiars by . . . treating them as he treats himself." Taoists say: "Regard your neighbor's gain as your own gain and regard your neighbor's loss as your own loss." In Islam: "None of you is a believer until he loves for his brother what he loves for himself." For Sikhs it is: "As thou deemest thyself so deem others. Then shalt thou become a partner in heaven." In Confucianism and Zoroastrianism the rule is stated in the same way as in the New Testament except that it is couched in negative terms: "Do not unto others what you would not they should do unto you." The Jewish equivalent in Leviticus 19:18 is "You shall love your neighbor as yourself."

There is no question but that we can take heart from this remarkable agreement regarding religious/ethical principles! Religion can indeed be a unifying influence in the world and in our personal relationships. What is unique about Christianity, however, is its special focus on the attitude we are to take toward our efforts to follow any rule. No religious tradition puts more emphasis on ethics than does the Christian faith. But it is precisely because of its high calling to do good and promote justice that the Christian Gospel addresses the problem of despair and discouragement. Great expectations can lead to even greater disappointments, so it is absolutely vital that we focus on our *attitude toward moral effort*. The radical Christian emphasis on the grace of God as revealed in the name of Jesus, makes it possible for us to combine our sense of moral urgency with a sense of humor and relaxation, because we know that ultimately everything does not rest on our shoulders alone. In this lies the difference that God makes in our lives: we can do our best to follow the Golden Rule (or any other ethical guidance), and to share our faith, not in a desperate or conceited attempt to save ourselves and the world, but in the cheerful confidence that God is forever channeling grace to all the world. The real Jesus Christ is the ultimate symbol and reality of this divine grace.

Down through the centuries Christians have used many grand and glorious images to praise Jesus. But nothing says it better than the hymn "All hail the power of Jesus' name!" — the name that means "God will save," "God heals," "God delivers." This name, *Jesus*, is the name above every name, because it is one with God's name. It is the source of theology that builds no doctrinal barriers. The love we see in Jesus is God's love, and the saving love and grace of God is all that we ever really need!

www.ingramcontent.com/pod-product-compliance
Lightning Source LLC
Chambersburg PA
CBHW060838050426
42453CB00008B/744